Franca Zambonini

TERESA OF CALCUTTA

A Pencil in God's Hand

TRANSLATED BY JORDAN AUMANN, OP

ALBA · HOUSE   **house**   NEW · YORK

SOCIETY OF ST. PAUL, 2187 VICTORY BLVD., STATEN ISLAND, NY 10314

A translation of *Teresa di Calcutta: La Matita di Dio*, published by Figlie di S. Paolo, Milano, and distributed by Commerciale Edizione Paoline, Torino, 1992.

Library of Congress Cataloging-in-Publication Data

Zambonini, Franca.
   [Teresa di Calcutta. English]
   Teresa of Calcutta : a pencil in God's hand / Franca Zambonini ;
  translated by Jordan Aumann.
      p.   cm.
   ISBN 0-8189-0670-7
   1. Teresa, Mother, 1910- . 2. Missionaries of Charity —
  Biography. 3. Nuns — India — Calcutta — Biography. 4. Missionaries
  of Charity — History. 5. Calcutta (India) — Biography. I. Title.
  BX4406.5.Z8Z3613   1993
  271'.97 — dc20   93-1046
  [B]   CIP

Produced and designed in the United States of America by the
Fathers and Brothers of the Society of St. Paul,
2187 Victory Boulevard, Staten Island, New York 10314,
as part of their communications apostolate.

ISBN: 0-8189-0670-7

Printing Information:

Current Printing - first digit	1	2	3	4	5	6	7	8	9	10

Year of Current Printing - first year shown

1993	1994	1995	1996	1997	1998

TERESA OF CALCUTTA

What we do is less than a drop in the ocean.
But without that drop,
the ocean would be lacking something.
I am a pencil in the hand of God.
He writes what he wants.

Mother Teresa

PREFACE

T his book is the result of an act of disobedience. Mother Teresa doesn't want anything written about her personally, but about "our people," meaning the poor. I have disobeyed her by making her the primary subject of this book. I trust that she will forgive me, with that same patience with which she has always received me, although, as she has said repeatedly and with some irony, she would rather bathe a leper than talk with a journalist. I am grateful to those who have agreed to talk to me about Mother Teresa. Father Celeste van Exem, her spiritual director, now old and sickly, performed the wearisome task of recalling past events during our lengthy conversations in the sultry heat of the afternoon in Calcutta. Michael Gomes, the government official who provided Mother Teresa with her first lodging, opened his home to me with the graciousness of bygone days. Sister Dionysia, a missionary in the slums of Calcutta, gladly agreed to interrupt her work for an entire day. John Raju, a leper in the colony of Titagarh, received me without any embarrassment and his wife Agnes offered me all that she had — a cup of goat's milk. Archbishop Henry D'Souza of Calcutta helped me to understand the "scandal" of India. Sister Rosario O'Reilly, a teacher in the school at Entally, recalled for me the period in which Mother Teresa had taught there. Father Zef Pllumi, a Franciscan from Tirana, Albania, who had been condemned to 23 years of forced labor, described the persecution that destroyed every trace of religion in Mother Teresa's native land. Glystina and Tolo Zhupa, a married couple from Tirana, told me of their friendship with Mother Teresa's mother and sister. Age Bojaxhiu Guttadauro Mancinelli, the only niece of Mother Teresa, overcame her initial reluctance and told me stories about the family. Dr. Vincenzo Giulio Bilotta, Mother Teresa's cardiologist, arranged for me to have numerous meetings with his famous patient.

Finally, I thank the following for their assistance: Father Leo Maasburg, who went to Erevan, Armenia, with the Missionaries of Charity after the earthquake; Gjon Sinishta, administrator at the University of San Francisco; Father Silvano Garrello, Salesian missionary; Maria Luisa and Massimo Croce and Sandra and Lorenzo Forzini, adoptive parents of Mother Teresa's infants; and all the Missionaries of Charity who were always available and willingly gave of their time to me.

Franca Zambonini

CONTENTS

Preface v
Introduction ix
Biographical Note xv
First Love 1
Beyond Every Wall 9
The Train to Darjeeling 21
Conviction 29
God's Vagabond 33
In Creek Lane 39
Life Is Life: Save It 53
Leprosy's Children 61
Missionaries to Prisons 71
The Scandal of India 83
Pioneer Scouts 95
The Commandos 105
The Poor Rich 117
The Smile of God 125
A Bad Heart 135
Graven on the Palms of My Hands 143
Lowly Servant 155
The Interview 161
Home at Last 173
After Mother Teresa? 185
Bibliography 189

INTRODUCTION

D ressed in a white sari with a border of three blue stripes and a small crucifix on the left shoulder, wearing a gray sweater against the cold and thin sandals on her naked feet, and carrying a cloth shopping-bag with wooden handles — that is how Mother Teresa arrived in Oslo to receive the Nobel prize and in New York to open a house for AIDS patients. That is also the way in which she appeared on the podium at the United Nations headquarters and amid the ruins of Beirut. In thousands of photographs she always looks the same, whether in the slums of a large city or in the offices and residences of the powerful and wealthy. There is a photo of Mother Teresa at the age of 15, taken in 1925 when she was known as Agnes Bojaxhiu and in the family was called by the pet name of Ganxha, the Albanian word for "flower bud." In the photo she is standing with her sister Age and the two girls look very much alike: bright eyes, high foreheads and prominent noses. They are wearing the Albanian national garb: embroidered vests and Turkish pantaloons. Each one has an arm around the other, with their heads close together. A half century later — in 1975 — *Time* magazine featured Mother Teresa on its cover. In an article entitled "Living Saints," Mother Teresa is portrayed with a deeply lined face in which the little eyes are somewhat sunken and the lips are tightly compressed. Her hair is covered with the edge of a sari which serves also as a veil. That has become the familiar icon of Mother Teresa of Calcutta.

Between the 1925 photo and the picture on *Time* magazine, decades of privation and exhausting labor have transformed the image of Mother Teresa into a symbol of universal charity. She has become a specialist in providing emergency relief whenever and wherever disaster strikes throughout the world. She describes her work as "love in action" or "something beautiful for God." Her mission is to the city streets, and it began when she first lifted a dying man from the sidewalk in Calcutta, violating the ancient Indian taboo of the "untouchables" and stirring the conscience of a fatalistic people. Since that time she has carried her apostolate to every continent. Mother Teresa has an obsession for the poor, for the wisdom of the poor. As she travels around the world, everything she sees relates in some way to poverty. For example, if on a flight her companion points out a beautiful lake down below, Mother Teresa clasps her hands together on her breast and says: "If only we could transport that lake to Ethiopia, where people are dying of thirst." In an age of materialistic atheism, she points to Christ as our guide and goal. An American journalist once saw her washing a man who was covered with sores and he exclaimed: "I would not do that for a million dollars!" Mother Teresa responded immediately: "Neither would I." And if anyone should criticize her because she spends her time dressing the wounds of the world instead of struggling to change the world, she would reply: "You change the world. In the meantime I shall nurse it." Mother Teresa can relate incidents that are both horrible and edifying. "I once picked up a man from the street and he was being eaten alive by worms. No one could bear to approach such a stench. As I bathed him, he asked me: 'Why are you doing this?' I answered: 'Because I love you.'" Mother Teresa will not permit her religious institute to be listed under the heading of charitable organizations or humanitarian institutions. "We are not an organization for social assistance. We strive to live a contemplative life. We contemplate Jesus in the Eucharist and Jesus in the poor who are abandoned by everyone."

* * * * *

Mother Teresa sometimes does things that are reactionary or even something of a scandal. We live in fear of sickness and disease and we refuse to accept death, but she walks among those who suffer from the most repugnant diseases, such as leprosy and AIDS. We surround ourselves with expensive and sometimes useless possessions, and in our homes we have the very latest domestic equipment. Mother Teresa, on the other hand, once commanded the Missionaries of Charity to get rid of the refrigerator, the vacuum cleaner and the carpets with which American Catholics had furnished a convent in San Francisco. In our society of waste, Mother Teresa sees the mountains of garbage that suffocate our cities as blasphemies against those who are deprived of everything. She says: "Poverty was not created by God. We have caused it — you and I — by our selfishness." Mother Teresa teaches the power of prayer. "The most important thing," she says, "is to pray, to pray, to pray." When faced with any difficulty, she advises her people to say a Hail Mary every morning. So many Hail Mary's can resolve everything. There is an Indian proverb that says: "Weave together the web of a spider and you can trap a tiger."

We surround ourselves with the machinery of technology but she favors manual labor, which is seen by some as a return to the Middle Ages. Each morning in the Motherhouse in Calcutta the Sisters fill the tank on the third floor of the building by carrying pails of water up the stairs instead of installing water pipes. In the midst of the noise of modern life, she chooses a monastic silence. "The trees, the flowers and the grass," she says, "grow in silence. The stars, the sun and the moon move in silence. Silence gives one a new way of looking at things." In an age that favors the gigantic, she loves little things. "What matters is not how much we do, but how much love we put in what we do. Little things done with great love."

Without possessing any particular oratorical skill, Mother

Teresa can hold the rapt attention of young people in a stadium, experts at an international congress, professors in the auditorium of a university, politicians in their parliaments. She does not prepare any notes nor does she follow any logical order. She describes her method as follows: "It is a martyrdom for me to speak in public. I close my eyes and I do this (then with her thumb she traces a little sign of the cross on her lips)." Pope John Paul II entrusted her with a special role in the evangelization and public relations of the Church when he told her: "You can go where I cannot go. Go and speak in my name."

The mere presence of Mother Teresa becomes a message. She herself is the word. As the American poet Walt Whitman said: "What you are speaks so loudly that I cannot hear what you say." She bears the weight of her popularity as a sacrifice, but she also reaps some spiritual profit from it: "With every photograph you take of me, a soul is saved." She possesses the highest intelligence: that of the heart. When she takes part in official ceremonies to receive awards, diplomas, honorary degrees or donations, the contrast between her and the other participants is always startling. The high-ranking officials are there in their dark, double-breasted suits, speaking with great self-confidence and discoursing in the rhetoric of officialdom. And there is Mother Teresa, bent over with arthritis, her head bowed, and saying only what is absolutely essential. She has no power or authority in those gatherings, but she achieves her purpose and she doesn't let anyone dominate her. She knows how to be intrepid and inflexible; her "no" is definitive and her "yes" is total.

The body of this woman of more than 80 years is emaciated as a result of her voluntary privations; her malfunctioning heart needs the help of a pace-maker; yet her dynamic energy exhausts the people around her. She never eats or drinks anything outside the convent, even when she is on a long journey; and she never accepts anything in the places she visits. This, she says, is "out of respect for the poor." Her nourishment consists of rice and vegetables; she drinks water or tea; she does not sleep more than three hours a night, taking time from rest in order "to work, to think of the Sisters, to answer letters, to do whatever is necessary." Her facial expression looks severe, but when the lines are extended in a smile, the light of grace spreads over her face.

She is a mystic, a contemplative, but at the same time she is a kindly administrator and zealous apostle of charity. Now her prestige and international reputation open all doors for her, but she began her work with only five rupees. From a Gypsy for God she has been transformed into an entrepreneur of charity. Millions of dollars pass through her hands, but she does not permit anyone to collect funds in her name. She doesn't beg; she waits, but she insists that the money donated should not come from superfluous funds. The donation should "hurt," so that the gift will first of all perfect the donor spiritually. Mother Teresa has inherited administrative acumen from her Albanian family of businessmen; and from India, the country of her adoption, she has imbibed a healthy fatalism. "We do everything for the Lord," she says. "It is up to him to think of us." This is the same answer she gives to those who ask what will happen to the Missionaries of Charity after her death. "If it is a work of God, he will take care of it. Otherwise it is just as well that it should disappear."

I have met the Missionaries of Charity in Calcutta, Manila, Rome, Melbourne, London, New York and Moscow. They are not all that numerous — only three thousand in the entire world — but they are very visible because, like Mother Teresa, they do not let the grass grow under their feet. All day long they travel about in pairs in search of the poor, reciting the rosary as they walk the city streets. Mother Teresa has instructed them: "We do not speak much; when we enter the houses of the poor, we take a broom and begin cleaning." She trains them in evangelical joy: "I don't want you to perform miracles in a harsh and severe manner; I prefer that you make mistakes with kindness." In all the houses of the Missionaries of Charity throughout the world, the words "I thirst" are always placed above the crucifix in the chapel in the local language. Those words of Christ on the cross are their manifesto.

There is a passage in the Gospel according to Luke which reads: "When you prepare a banquet, invite beggars and the crippled, the lame and the blind. You should be pleased that they cannot repay you, for you will be repaid in the resurrection of the just" (Lk 14:13-14). Mother Teresa has invited to her banquet only those who cannot repay her. She has said: "Some people demonstrate for justice and human rights. We have no time for that. There are too many human beings who are dying of hunger and are deprived of love. In people such as these we serve Jesus twenty-four hours of the day."

BIOGRAPHICAL NOTE

I n this book I have recounted some of the events in the life of Mother Teresa, but not all; that would have required a much larger volume. I have described only those events that I have witnessed personally or have been related to me by other persons who witnessed them. Moreover, this book is not a biography and for that reason I have not followed a strictly chronological order. Consequently, the following biographical outline will be useful for those who are interested in knowing the important dates in the life of Mother Teresa and in the religious institute of the Missionaries of Charity that she founded.

1910   Agnes Gonxha Bojaxhiu is born of Albanian parents at Skopje, the capital of Macedonia in Yugoslavia, which at that time was part of the Ottoman Empire. Her father, Nikola, was a wealthy merchant and was active in the movement for the liberation of Albania from the Turks. Her mother, Drana, was a courageous woman. After the premature death of her husband, she raised three children: Lazar, Agnes and Age. She provided them with religious instruction and an education on a par with that of their peers.

1928   At the age of 18, on September 25, Agnes leaves Skopje for Ireland and is accepted by the Sisters of Loreto, the Irish branch of the Institute of the Blessed

Virgin Mary, founded by Mary Ward in 1609. The Sisters of Loreto concentrate especially on sending missionaries to India, and Agnes had dreamed of going to India since she first heard some Yugoslav missionaries speak of it.

1928   On December 1, now a novice with the name Sister Mary Teresa of the Child Jesus, Agnes sails for India on the ship "Marcha," together with Betika Kajnc, a Yugoslav named Sister Mary Magdalen. They arrive at Colombo on December 27, and on January 6 Sister Mary Teresa begins her novitiate training at Darjeeling, in the foothills of the Himalayas.

1931   Sister Mary Teresa pronounces her first vows at Darjeeling on May 24 and she will make her final religious profession on May 24, 1937. Until August of 1948 she teaches geography and religion at St. Mary's College at Entally, Calcutta, and eventually becomes director of the school.

1946   During the night of September 10, while travelling by train to Darjeeling, she feels called to serve the poorest of the poor. It is a "vocation within a vocation." She consults with her spiritual director, Father Celeste van Exem, and with the Archbishop of Calcutta, Ferdinand Perier. They both advise patience and caution.

1948   Sister Mary Teresa writes to the Congregation for Religious in Rome on February 7, asking permission to leave the Sisters of Loreto and dedicate herself exclusively to the poor of India. On receiving an affirmative response to her request, Sister Mary Teresa replaces the black habit of the Sisters of Loreto with the white sari of the Indian poor and leaves the convent. Alone, she departs for Patna to take up nurse's training at the hospital of the American

Medical Missionaries. Three months later she returns to Calcutta and lodges for a time with the Little Sisters of the Poor. By December of this year she opens a little school in Moti Jihl, one of the poorest sections of Calcutta.

1949   On February 6 she moves to a lodging provided for her by the Gomes family, Number 14 on Creek Lane. She is still alone, but on the feast of St. Joseph, March 19, the first postulant arrives. She is a former student of Sister Mary Teresa at Entally, a Bengali girl named Subashini Das. For her religious name she takes Agnes, the baptismal name of Sister Mary Teresa.

1950   The Congregation of the Missionaries of Charity is approved at Calcutta on October 7, and in the following years the most famous foundations are made: Nirmal Hriday, the house for the dying; Shishu Bhavan, the house for infants; and Shanti Nagar, the lepers' village.

1960   In October of this year Mother Teresa leaves India for the first time in 32 years. She is invited to the United States to attend a congress. Before returning to Calcutta, she stops in Rome to ask Pope John XXIII, through the good offices of Cardinal Gregory Agagianian, to recognize the Missionaries of Charity as a congregation of pontifical right. Also at Rome she meets her brother Lazar, whom she has not seen since she was 18 years old.

1965   On February 1 the Missionaries of Charity becomes a congregation of pontifical right and Mother Teresa is able to open houses outside of India. On July 26 a house is founded at Cocorote in Venezuela. It is the first of 443 houses established in 95 different countries.

1968 Pope Paul VI invites Mother Teresa to found a house in Rome.

1971 The first Pope John XXIII Peace Prize is awarded to Mother Teresa by Pope Paul VI.

1979 Mother Teresa is awarded the Nobel Peace Prize in Oslo, Norway, on December 10. This is the most prestigious of all the honors that she has received.

1990 After suffering several heart attacks in the previous year, Mother Teresa is hospitalized for a time and she offers her resignation as Superior General to Pope John Paul II. However, the General Chapter of the Congregation re-elects her unanimously on September 8, and Mother Teresa accepts.

1991 On March 31 Mother Teresa re-opens the cathedral at Tirana, Albania, which had been converted into a movie house during the dictatorship of Enver Hoxha. She also opens three houses in her native land of Albania, thus realizing one of her life's dreams.

FIRST LOVE

A whiff of strong disinfectant catches at the throat as soon as the door of Nirmal Hriday is opened. It is the Home for the Dying in the Kalighat section of Calcutta. *Kali* is the black goddess of the Hindus and the ancient and venerated temple in her honor is situated in this quarter of the city. The word *ghat* signifies the place of cremation. In fact, the funeral pyres are but a short distance away, on the banks of the river. In the morning the fumes of cremation hover over the city and mingle with the perfume of the flower wreaths placed at the foot of the goddess by the pilgrims. But for the moment the odor of disinfectant dominates everything.

A Missionary of Charity peeps through the door and I give her the letter of introduction from Sister Michael Joseph, the superior of the Motherhouse. The Missionary reads it and then bids me enter. She is very young and efficient. "Put your things here," she says. I put my purse on a little stand and when I turn around the Sister has disappeared.

A sign on the wall reads: "Welcome to the Home for the Dying, the first love of Mother Teresa." The silence and dim light are like that in the water of a deep pool. A milky light filters through an arabesque grill and gradually one's eyes become adjusted. Then I see. The patients are lying on iron cots arranged in two rows on raised pavement, and there is an aisle down the middle at a slightly lower level.

A male volunteer with a red beard is dunking a small piece of bread in milk and placing it in the toothless mouth of a patient. A Missionary Brother is moving the cot of a patient who is nothing but skin and bones beneath the bed sheet. A Sister squats on the pavement as she dresses wounds, holding a pair of tweezers in which there is a piece of cotton soaked in red disinfectant.

All this is done quietly and gently; the atmosphere is somewhat melancholy. Unimaginable misfortunes have brought human beings here to die, their skin taut over their bones, their mouths open and gasping for air, the cords of their necks stretched tight, their cheeks sunken. The dying are sacred to all religions, but here they can pass through the gate to eternity comforted by loving hands and blessed by the rites of their religion. A few drops of water from the Ganges River are placed in the mouth of the Hindus; a verse from the Koran is read to the Muslims; the Christians are anointed with holy oil. For those who belong to no religion, the face of a Missionary of Charity bends over them to give witness to the love of God for all his creatures.

* * * * *

Mother Teresa has frequently described the first time that she rescued from the street a dying woman whose body had been gnawed at by rats and bitten by ants. She hoisted the woman on her shoulders and carried her to the nearest hospital, but the attendants refused to accept her. Mother Teresa stood her ground, immovable, at the entrance to the hospital. She would not leave until the woman was admitted. Then and there she decided that human beings have the right to die with dignity even in the hell of Calcutta. She went to the Commissioner of Health and asked that he give her a place where a person could die with dignity. All she wanted was a place; she and her Sisters would take care of the rest. The Commissioner was Doctor Ahmed, and when Mother Teresa requested anything, it was impossible to refuse. He offered her a semi-abandoned building

2

near the temple of the goddess Kali. At one time it had been used as a *darmashalah*, a lodging for pilgrims to the temple.

In his book *Tristes Tropiques*, Claude Levi-Strauss describes the building as it was before Mother Teresa transformed it into the Home for the Dying: "It resembled a covered marketplace. It was a lengthy building made of cement and divided into two sections, one for men and the other for women. On either side of the length of the building there were two raised cement platforms, destined for beds.... When the pilgrims awoke in the morning and went to the temple to pray for a cure, the floors were washed clean with strong jets of water and prepared for the next group of pilgrims. Never, except in concentration camps, were human beings treated so much like meat in a slaughter-house."

It was in 1952 that Mother Teresa accepted the building offered by Doctor Ahmed and took possession of the *darmashalah* at the temple of Kali. The long-abandoned building was cleansed of its filth by a squad of Sisters, and Mother Teresa named it Nirmal Hriday, which in Bengali means Immaculate Heart, so named because the day of its inauguration, August 22, was at that time the feast of the Immaculate Heart of Mary.

* * * * *

One does not feel any anxiety or fear when visiting the Home for the Dying, but one would prefer not to be there or at least to walk around on tiptoe. To me it seems almost pitiless to stand there and watch someone die. I go in search of the Sister who has let me in and I find her bent over a cot, holding up her right arm to give a blood transfusion. She looks at me, twisting her head to one side; she cannot straighten up because of the short tube connected to the container of blood. I ask her: "What should I do?"

My question must have seemed badly timed. She lowers her head once more and with her free arm she makes a circular motion. I understand her to mean: "Look around. There is plenty to do." I panic for a moment, and then on the wall in front of me I see a crucifix with broken legs. A printed sign says: "Let my hands heal thy broken body."

Lord, I would like to heal your broken body. With all my heart I would like to do so. But to do it, I would have to bathe that trembling human body, feed that drooling mouth, touch that forehead bathed in the sweat of death's agony. I have nothing to do with this antechamber of death; I only asked permission to visit this place.

The fans cool the perspiring patients and diffuse the odor of disinfectant. The Sister pays no attention to me, nor do the volunteers who are busy with their tasks. I hasten to get my purse and I grasp it tightly to re-assume my proper role. I am here as a journalist and not as a volunteer. After all, I am not Sally.

* * * * *

I met Sally this morning at Mass at the Motherhouse on Lower Circle Road. Anybody can attend Mass there; the address and the schedule are actually printed on the city map of Calcutta, together with information about museums and places of interest to tourists. The *Sikh* taxi driver, who took me there from the hotel while it was still dark, wrapped his turban around his head and prepared to catch up on his sleep while he waited for me. I rang the bell at the front gate and followed the silent procession that was ascending the stairs to the chapel on the second floor. Boys and girls and a middle-aged couple, all foreigners, left their shoes at the door and entered the chapel in their stocking feet. They then genuflected on the matting near the long line of Missionaries of Charity.

Mother Teresa is squatting on the floor in her accustomed place near the door. She remains absorbed in prayer throughout the entire Mass, her hands clasped together and resting on her chest. The long, narrow chapel is illumined by ten light bulbs, and as the light of day enters through the large windows little by little, Mother now and then reaches up to the switch on the wall and extinguishes a few of the lights. By the end of the Mass she has extinguished them all, because by then the bright sunshine has invaded the chapel. Though immersed in conversation with God, Mother Teresa does not neglect the little tasks of daily life.

At the end of the Mass we gather in the corridor and Mother Teresa greets me immediately. Then, with solicitude and a touch of affable irony, she says: "It was an early rising for you, wasn't it? Go down and have some tea." She then hurries over to the young American couple who were on their honeymoon and wanted her blessing.

The Sisters were already in the courtyard. They had put their saris in soapy water before Mass and now they were washing them. Each barefooted Sister, with sleeves rolled up above the elbow, was bent over her own pail. All the Missionaries of Charity throughout the whole world perform that same task every morning. Each Sister has two saris, and I remembered the saying of the Venetian Count who carried only two shirts in his luggage: "Una adosso; una nel fosso" (One on my back and one in the wash).

Cups of tea were ready and waiting in the parlor above the courtyard. Each cup was different from the others and some of them were chipped. The tea was black and hot, without sugar, milk or lemon, English style. "It settles the empty stomach," says a girl standing next to me. It is Sally, a high school teacher from Ireland. Each year she spends her vacation in Calcutta and works in the Home for the Dying. This time she has been able to spend six months in India. I asked her if she had spent all that time in Calcutta. "Not spent but profited," she corrected me. She is a bit sad because next week she must return to Ireland.

"Come to Kalighat," she urged. "Today will be a quiet day because we finished the cleaning yesterday. Ask permission from Sister Michael Joseph."

* * * * *

Down on Lower Circle Road the noise of the traffic has not disturbed the sleep of the *Sikh* taxi driver. I had to shake him to wake him up, and his eyes were still heavy with sleep when he dropped me off at Kalighat in front of the temple of the goddess Kali.

The temple stands in the center of a block of buildings and is surmounted with spires fashioned in the Bengali style. The area around Kalighat is a gathering place for pilgrims and it bustles with the usual morning activities. Goats browse in the piles of refuse; crows are perched on the tops of the vendors' shops, which are no bigger than large boxes; children are playing hop-scotch, jumping with joined feet inside squares that have been marked on the ground with chalk.

No sooner do I get out of the taxi than I am besieged by vendors of garlands of hibiscus and little statues of the goddess Kali; by women selling packets of leaves wrapped around a slice of cucumber; by beggars who show me their wounds or the stump of a limb and beg for alms; by teenagers who know a smattering of English and offer themselves as tourist guides. The pressure of the insistent crowd takes one's breath away.

With the help of the taxi driver, who is fortified by his title as a *Sikh* and his tall stature, I succeed in making my way through the crowd. But it is not yet eight o'clock, and a sign on the door of the Home for the Dying requests that the bell not be rung before nine o'clock. That gives me time to look around.

In the center of the courtyard of the temple I see the huge statue, surrounded by the pilgrims who are jostling one another in order to touch it. The face of the goddess is painted black, a red tongue protrudes from her mouth, a third eye is implanted in her forehead, and she has four arms. One hand holds a dagger, another holds up a severed bloody head, and the remaining two hands are raised in benediction over the faithful. Around the neck there is a necklace of snakes and another one of skulls.

A dignified gentleman, wearing the white robe of a Brahmin, approaches me. He greets me politely and asks if he can help me with an explanation.

"My name is Manih Chatterjii. I am a priest of this temple, which is the most ancient in Calcutta and is the heart of Hinduism. Kali is the Great Mother, the goddess of power, of creation, of destruction and of conservation. She destroys evil and preserves life. We also call her *Durga*, which means 'inaccessible.' We celebrate her feast, *Kali pujah*, between October 10 and 20. Every Hindu is obliged to make a pilgrimage to this shrine at least once in a lifetime.

"Calcutta owes its name to the goddess Kali: *Kali-kuta* means the place of Kali. One must enter the temple with an empty stomach and after having bathed. Look at the large crowd that is already here at this morning hour. But you, *memsahib*, cannot enter now because I presume you have already had breakfast and have not gone through the ritual bathing. Return tomorrow, fasting, and you can perform the ablutions in the pool behind the temple.

"After your visit you can partake of *fedda*, our sweets made of condensed milk, flour and sugar. You can also get some of the religious prints decorated with orange-colored symbols, the same that Kali has. Married women paint them on their foreheads to signify: *Long life with my husband*. You may also offer Kali a wreath of hibiscus; red is the color used to destroy the evil devils. But you must not smell the perfume of the flowers; that fragrance is reserved for the goddess.

"Come, and I shall show you our kitchens, where each day we prepare 500 cakes for the poor. Yes, I know; you are a Christian. We are friends of the Christians. We have good neighborly relations with Mother Teresa, who works in this same building. Good-bye until tomorrow."

* * * * *

By this time it is nine o'clock, so I knock at the door of Nirmal Hriday, am mistaken for a volunteer and feel embarrassed. I wander through the section reserved for women. They are lying motionless on their cots and are being cared for by the Sisters wearing the sari, the Missionary Brothers in blue shirts, and the volunteers dressed in checkered green aprons. I ask for

Sally, the teacher from Ireland, who should have arrived by now. "She was here a moment ago," says a volunteer who is on her knees, mopping the floor with a rag. From behind a curtain comes the sound of conversation, but so low that it is little more than a whisper. I pull the curtain aside and there is Sally. With a soapy sponge she is washing the body of an old lady who is as thin as a featherless bird, with shoulder blades protruding like wings. Sally bathes the woman as gently and delicately as a mother bathes her newborn infant, all the while speaking to her in English, to which the woman responds in Hindu. How they are able to understand each other, I don't know, nor can I imagine what they can possibly be saying to each other. Mother Teresa once wrote: "At Nirmal Hriday no one dies depressed, despairing, neglected, without food or without love. That is why I think that this is the most precious house in Calcutta. We give the poor what they ask, according to their religion. Some ask for water from the Ganges River; still others for a word or a prayer. Some ask only for an apple, a piece of bread or a cigarette. Yet others want only someone near them. We help them to make their peace with God. We live now so that they can die and return to their true homeland, as it is written in the book, whether it be the book of the Hindus, the Muslims, the Buddhists, the Catholics, the Protestants or those of any other religion."

* * * * *

The chapel in the Home for the Dying is under the roof, and from there one can see the pilgrims to the goddess Kali assembled in the inner courtyard. The hubbub of the milling crowd rises up to the terraced roof, together with the sultry air from the courtyard. The chapel welcomes me as a cool and quiet refuge. To the right of the altar hangs a crucifix, and above it are the words: "I thirst."

You thirst, O Lord, and I have not given you anything to drink....

BEYOND EVERY WALL

There are walls everywhere in India. The poor are separated from the rich, the sick from the healthy, the people on the street from those who work in offices and factories. Perhaps the contrasts are nowhere as great as in Calcutta, where, in the words of Kipling, one finds "palace, byre and hovel — poverty and pride — side by side."

I have seen the sanitary wall that surrounds the colony of lepers. At one of these colonies in Titagarh, a mother called out to her two naked children with shaved heads, who were standing in the sewage drain, not to get into trouble. A guard standing on the other side of the wall had waved his long bamboo stick at the children.

I have passed through the wall of the enclosure into the palaces of the *maharajah* and the *rajah*, the ex-leaders of the Hindu religion, and the *nawah* and the *nizam*, the ex-leaders of the Muslim religion. In the reception area of the Maharani, where guests in red chiffon saris bordered in gold were gathered, I walked and conversed with the pilot of a MIG from the Indian air force. A servant in an orange-colored garb followed us with a silver ashtray so that the ashes of our cigarettes would not fall on the neatly trimmed lawn.

I have also lived behind a wall of indifference, because it is necessary to keep one's eyes, ears and mouth closed if one is to survive in a city of three thousand squalid huts. Anyone born in

Calcutta learns from childhood how to protect oneself in this way. One morning I met a child dressed in a blue jacket and yellow tie. He was on his way to school and was followed by a servant carrying a violin. The child's hair was neatly combed and parted on his head like the wings of a crow. As he walked along the sidewalk, he zig-zagged his way through the crowd without looking at them or even brushing against them. He seemed to be guided by some kind of radar similar to that of a bat.

There was also a wall between Mother Teresa and the poor when, shortly after her religious profession, she began teaching the students at St. Mary's High School, and again when she changed the black habit of a Sister of Loreto for the sari of an Indian of the lowest class. The word "wall" even crops up in Mother Teresa's conversation: "Our Sisters must walk on the street, take the streetcar as our people do, and enter the houses of the poor. We cannot enclose ourselves behind walls and wait for the poor to knock at our door."

Someone suggested that Mother Teresa should open permanent institutions such as orphanages, hospices and hospitals, where the Sisters could be occupied full time inside the building. Mother Teresa said no: "Others can do that type of work much better than we. Our work is outside, outside the walls, where other Congregations do not go."

At another time she said: "We are street people. Our Sisters walk the streets and they pray as they walk. Sometimes to tell me how much time it took to reach a place, they tell me how many rosaries they said — three rosaries, four rosaries. They walk so rapidly that in Calcutta they are called 'the racing Sisters'."

* * * * *

In the Entally section of Calcutta a wall three meters high separates the grounds of St. Mary's High School from the slum area of Moti Jheel, a dust-covered conglomeration of huts that are firmly secured by mud, straw and hemp. The gate that connects these two worlds is decorated with the shield of the school: a red heart with a white cross and a white heart pierced with a red arrow. The uniforms of the students are also red and white.

Outside the emblazoned gate the street is choked with a never-ending flow of traffic and pedestrians. A policeman in a colonial helmet tries in vain to control it by waving his stick. Rickshaws slip silently through the crowds at a speed depending on the age and strength of the human horses panting between the poles.

On the sidewalk that runs along the wall a woodcutter is busy splitting tree trunks. He strips off the bark, gathers the pieces of wood and the splinters and chips, and stacks them neatly into piles, each one with its price. They are then sold as kindling wood to the homeless people who cook their meals on the side of the street.

Nearby a boy cuts lengthwise the shells of coconuts, which are used for polishing the floors, as is done in many Oriental countries. Then there is a Missionary of Charity, a familiar figure on the streets of Calcutta; she has set up a stand for the monthly distribution of medicine for the lepers of the quarter, who are waiting patiently in line. The Sister holds a packet of cards that specify the prescribed dosage of medicine. She fills the prescriptions and then distributes the bottles of medicine to the patients.

Behind the entrance gate of the high school there is a beautiful lawn of Irish green. It looks as if the gardener has cut the grass this morning and watered the magnolias around the cricket court. The yellow varnish of the pagoda that houses the statue of St. Therese looks as if it had recently been retouched.

Only the crows call attention to the scene with their discordant cries. In India the crows fly into the houses and rob whatever glitters. To prevent this, the Sisters have put grates on the windows. Once the monsoon winds blew down a tree and in its empty trunk was found a treasure of rings and trinkets that had been stored there by these flying thieves.

* * * * *

Mother Teresa had worked and taught for 19 years in this little paradise of St. Mary's High School, from 1929 to 1948. Sister Rosario O'Reilly, 73 years old, whose strong Irish face is illumined by two bright blue eyes, is the only Sister at Entally who had known Mother Teresa. Seated on a park bench in the shade of a mango tree, she told me about those days.

> At that time the habit of our Sisters of Loreto was black and we wore a black veil. After the Second Vatican Council we made a change. Now the habit is blue in the winter and in the summer it is white with a blue veil.
>
> Our Congregation was founded by Mary Ward in England in 1609. The Irish branch was established in 1821 in the abbey of Our Lady of Loreto at Rathfarnham by Teresa Ball. She sent the first Sisters of Loreto to India in 1841. There the Sisters dedicated themselves to teaching, with a strong missionary zeal. In 1976 our Motherhouse was transferred from Rathfarnham to Rome.

* * * * *

There is a photo taken in the 1930's which Mother Teresa sent to her mother, her sister Age and her aunt Maria. She is shown with some of the other Sisters of Loreto in the convent parlor at Entally. The Sisters are dressed in the black habit and veil. The younger ones are standing and the older ones are seated on wicker chairs, their hands clasped on their laps. Behind the group is a statue of an angel. One can visualize a convent of cool rooms, shaded corridors, the odor of good food in the dining room, and all the conveniences of a well-ordered and comfortable life. All this is far removed from the suffering and misery of Calcutta. Where are the sick, the disfigured lepers, the human rejects, the undernourished babies, the worn-out women of that nightmare of a city? As yet the Sister from Albania knows nothing of these things. She had only a glimpse of them on her arrival, when she disembarked in India on December 27, 1928, after a four-week sea voyage with her companions, the Yugoslav Sister Mary Magdalen Kajnc and the Irish Sister Joyce Berchmans. This is the way she describes her first impressions of India in a letter sent to the Yugoslav missionary magazine, *Katolicke Misije*:

> We arrived on December 27 and a Mr. Scalon, a brother of one of our Sisters, was there to meet us. We immediately observed with great astonishment how life is lived on the street.... Most of the men were half naked. Their smooth, glossy skin and thick hair were conspicuous under the boiling sun. It tugged at one's heartstrings to see men pulling rickshaws as if they were horses. We decided that we would never ride in those vehicles. And what happened? At that very moment Mr. Scalon made us depart in one of them. We were paralyzed! We tried to make our weight as light as possible....

One's first impression of Calcutta is soon mitigated. Less than three weeks after her arrival — on January 16, 1929 — the little Albanian Sister, who had but recently completed her eighteenth year, was sent to the novitiate in Darjeeling. Sister Rosario O'Reilly describes it with understandable pride:

> Our house at Darjeeling stands on a hill covered with flowering bushes, and at its base there is a garden that

is so luxurious that many tourists enter our property rather than visit the nearby botanical garden.

Darjeeling is the queen of all the mountain resorts in India. It stands at the foot of the Himalayas and is surrounded by fragrant fields of tea plants. In the background the snow-covered mountain peaks are set against the blue of the sky. One can reach the summit in nine hours on a little train painted blue. It is a marvel of railroad engineering, travelling upward in dizzying curves on the highest railroad tracks in the world, through forests of magnolias and rhododendrons.

Darjeeling was a popular resort for the English, who built their summer homes there to escape the scorching heat of Calcutta. It looks like the London of the Victorian period, populated with Indian faces. Tourists go there to breathe the pure air, to visit the Himalayan museum and the zoo, where one can see red pandas, white Siberian tigers, and the ever-patient yak, the ox with a hump on its shoulders.

* * * * *

The mistress of novices at that time was Sister Baptista Murphy, a capable woman of strong character and high principles. She knew how to direct the novices first to prayer and the spiritual life and then to the apostolate. Under her guidance Sister Teresa made her first religious profession on May 24, 1931. She made her final profession on May 24, 1937.

In the register of the novitiate at Darjeeling, now preserved at the convent in Entally, Sister Teresa had written her name in various ways: Bojaotis, Bojadijevic, and Boyagis. Sister Rosario O'Reilly explained this phenomenon by noting the difficulty in translating the Albanian name into English. In the end the correct spelling was accepted as Bojaxhiu. "But this is of little importance," said Sister Rosario.

As she recalls, Sister Teresa did not manifest any extraordinary gifts, except that she was very active and dedicated. "She did not spare herself either in work or in the exercises of piety." She was a joyful person, always ready to enjoy a joke, sometimes doubling up with laughter. In the face of a difficulty she would encourage the Sisters with the following strange saying: "We are peaceful and we shall die peaceful." She was also definite and firm in her ideas. She learned Hindu and Bengali very quickly, after learning English at Rathfarnham in Ireland. She taught Hindu to the newly arrived Sisters, using a simple method: they had to memorize six sentences each day. She also taught geography and catechism to the students in the courses for the certificate of elementary teachers.

When, in 1944, the superior became ill, Sister Teresa replaced her temporarily as superior and director of the school. "Those years were very difficult," says Sister Rosario. "Food was rationed and the work was constantly increasing. Sister Teresa, whose health was never robust, came down with tuberculosis. Consequently, when I heard that she had left our community to work on the streets with the poor, I wondered if her constitution could withstand such a challenging life that was lacking in everything."

* * * * *

The bell rings for the recreation period and crowds of students swarm into the park. The little ones chase after one another; the older ones walk around arm in arm or gather in little groups animated with laughter. There are 1,600 students in the school, both commuters and boarding students, comprising the elementary school and the high school. The majority are of the Hindu religion, but there is a good number of Catholics and a small number of Muslims. The uniforms are red and white, the colors of the shield of the Sisters of Loreto. The short-haired little girls in the elementary school wear a red blouse of Indian design and a white belt; the girls in the middle school wear white with

15

a red belt and a red ribbon in their black tresses; the older girls in the higher classes wear a white sari with a red border and their long hair hangs loose. The classroom in which Mother Teresa taught is now the room for grade 5-B and it is in the oldest part of the building, near the pond. Sister Rosario points out the new desks but the teacher's desk is from former times and the varnish is peeling somewhat. It is the hour for the English class, which is taught by a distinguished Bengali lady named Swarna Datta. She feels very honored to occupy the post that once belonged to Mother Teresa. She calls it the "Nobel Prize." Sister Rosario O'Reilly came to teach at St. Mary's School in 1947, which was a tragic year for Calcutta because that city was the center of the revolts that preceded Indian independence. Mahatma Gandhi, the "Great Soul," the apostle of non-violence, organized spectacular hunger strikes. That was a paradoxical move in a country of famished people, but it was the only political weapon available to a defenseless people against the guns of the English. Calcutta was torn by the violence of Hindu and Muslim extremists and the echoes of those tragic events reverberated even within the walls of St. Mary's School in Entally. Deaf to all admonitions, the girls also organized protest strikes. Finally, Mother Teresa exerted her authority; she spoke to the most influential students and was able to avert further disorders until India won its independence on August 15, 1947.

* * * * *

Meanwhile, it is very likely that Sister Teresa was gradually moving toward a decision. She continued to teach the girls. She who would later cause the entire world to speak of her, worked silently and in obedience to the regulations. Faithful to her daily duties and secure in the comfortable life of the convent, she must have thought frequently of the poor on the filthy streets of Calcutta. Sister Teresa continued to teach at St. Mary's School until August 17, 1948, and on August 18 she said good-bye to the school and convent of the Sisters of Loreto. She left the security and protection of her conventual cell, the aroma of the good food in the refectory, the cooling breezes from the fans, the affection of the students, the joys of community recreation, and the laughter that made her double over. She "leaped over the wall," retaining only the name "Mother Teresa," which had been hers since she became superior. She was 38 years old and at last, according to the phrase of Pindaro, "she became what she was." Her infancy and youth in Skopje, Albania, the time spent at Rathfarnham, the novitiate at Darjeeling and the teaching at Entally — it all coalesced in a radical and definitive decision. It was an imperative that only an authentically mystical soul could obey without trembling.

The woman who "leaped over the wall" is not the least bit sentimental; she is energetic, disciplined and patient, and also daring. Perhaps she was as yet unaware of her tremendous power that would revolutionize the world. But they were badly mistaken who interpreted her departure as a rash action or as desertion, and expected that she would soon return to the fold like a repentant lamb. Sister Rosario has her own personal idea concerning the reasons for Mother Teresa's decision, although Mother herself always attributed it to an inspiration she received on the night of September 10, 1946, during a trip to Darjeeling. This is Sister Rosario's interpretation:

> I believe that Mother Teresa had discovered the poor long before that, when the great drought hit Bengali in 1943. During that year the girls of wealthy families who owned houses and property at Dacca or other localities not affected by the drought, left Calcutta. The school was closed; it remained open only for the poor students, and they attended free of charge. Many of these students came to school with stomachs bloated because of the lack of food. The Sisters provided them with lunch insofar as they were able. I

17

believe that it was that situation that awakened in Mother Teresa the first impulse to dedicate herself to the poor. Later, of course, she had a vocation within a vocation, but in my opinion the roots of that call are to be found in the great suffering she witnessed at the time of the great drought.

Mother Teresa's recruits in her new form of life were ex-students from St. Mary's. Sister Rosario had known many of them. The first was Subashini Das, who became a Missionary of Charity under the name of Sister Agnes. Others were Bridget Francis, Magdalen Gomes, Kiron Dutta, and some who had assisted her at the beginning. Thus, Lotika Katre later became a teacher at St. Mary's and Martha Anjos joined the Sisters of Loreto with the name Sister Francesca. "I know," said Sister Rosario, with a trace of pride in her Congregation, "that Mother Teresa once said: 'In my heart I belong to Loreto.' She then added that she would not be able to face God if she had not answered his call."

* * * * *

Years later, an American friend and collaborator of Mother Teresa, named Eileen Egan, had an opportunity to accompany Mother on a visit to a former fellow teacher in the school at Entally. Eileen describes it as follows in her book, *Such a Vision of the Street*:

Mother Teresa still maintained family ties with the Loreto Sisters. One day, returning from Moti Jihl, we went through the wide gates of the Loreto compound in Entally. Entering St. Mary's School, we were greeted by an old Sister on duty who remembered Mother Teresa from the days just over a decade earlier when she was headmistress of the school. There were no students about, since it was holiday time.

The old Sister said she still thought about Mother Teresa, and what made her happy was that Mother Teresa still thought about Entally and took time to pay a visit. As we walked along the corridor and into the office that had been Mother Teresa's as headmistress of St. Mary's, I marveled at the brightness of the polished floors, a special brightness achieved only in floors in convents. In those classrooms, Mother Teresa had inspired young women with a love of goodness and a compassion for the poor, in addition to imparting knowledge that would be called for on examination papers. In the sacristy of the impressive chapel, she had brought her first cheap sari to be blessed.

Always purposeful, Mother Teresa soon hurried me out of the compound. As we went through the gates, I thought of the unprecedented courage it took for Sister Teresa to walk through those gates one evening in August a decade ago, after having laid aside a garb that had been part of her life for nineteen years. One day, in talking about the days at St. Mary's, she made a casual remark: "The love the students had for me and the influence I had over them for good — it was nothing I could take pride in. It was God using me."

THE TRAIN TO DARJEELING

The Jesuits have labored in India for centuries. The most famous is Father Robert de Nobili, who died on January 12, 1656, after preaching the Gospel in India for 50 years. He wore the garb of a Brahmin and his only distinguishing mark was a small cross on his chest. He followed the Indian customs, and his one meal a day consisted of rice, milk and some vegetables. He was intensely interested in Hindu mysticism. Several Jesuits assisted Mother Teresa when she decided to leave the Sisters of Loreto to dedicate herself to the service of the poorest of the poor. Father Robert Antoine, who later became chaplain at the Home for the Dying at Kalighat, was a professor at the university. He read to his students the great epic poem of India, *Mahabharata* and Dante's *The Divine Comedy*. He also composed hymns in Bengali, writing the words and accompanying them with the rhythm of the *tablas*, the local drums. Father Peter Fallon, a student of Hindu spirituality, was the first one to approve of Mother Teresa's choice of the sari as the garb of the Missionaries of Charity. Ferdinand Perier, Archbishop of Calcutta, advised her to be prudent and patient but at the same time he supported her courageously. Father Julien Henry instructed the first Missionaries of Charity, and Father Celeste van Exem became Mother Teresa's spiritual director. Father van Exem was born on October 4, 1908, and had lived in India for 52 years. Thanks to his help, Mother Teresa was able to overcome the initial difficulties and to found the religious institute of the Missionaries of Charity. He also wrote the first little chronicle of the work of Mother Teresa, which was published in the local daily paper, *The Calcutta Statesman*. That article was the forerunner of the thousands of articles that were to establish the fame of the Albanian Sister who had become an Indian citizen.

At this writing, Father Celeste van Exem is confined to his bed on the third floor of St. Xavier's College, the Jesuit University on Park Street. I visited him in the early part of the evening. It is the hour in which the Calcutta of the wealthy and the Calcutta of high finance and computers is preparing for the activities of the evening. On that particular evening a VIP could not afford to miss the reception in honor of Ajit Kerker, the chairman of the Taj Group of hotels, a chain of the most luxurious hotels in all India. The cost of a room per person for one night is equivalent to a year's salary for an Indian of the middle class. The Maharaja and the Maharani, the foreign diplomats, the import-export businessmen, the stars of movies, theater and dance — they will all be present.

It is also the hour in which the workers leave their place of employment and pass through the lines of shoeshine boys who knock their brushes against the containers of shoe polish to attract attention. The vendors of mangoes, melons and papayas do a good business. For one rupee you can buy a slice of fruit to provide some relief from the sultry heat of the late afternoon.

It is also the hour in which the Calcutta of the streets gets ready for the night. The homeless stretch out on the sidewalks and wrap themselves in their *dhoti*, a covering resembling a shroud, in which they sleep as immobile as a corpse. The breathing of each one, multiplied by thousands, becomes the breathing of the city that rests, exhausted after the day's activities.

* * * * *

This particular evening Father Celeste van Exem is happy because the doctor has told him that he will amputate only Father's big toe and not the entire leg, as he had previously intended. The gangrene has been checked, and although the legs are black as far as the knees, they can be saved. Father Celeste is finally able to talk about the rats that had bit him during his sleep and poisoned his blood. "They were rats belonging to a family of merchants named Malvalis, who took good care of them. The family must have been away on vacation because the rats attacked me with extraordinary voracity." This happened at St. Francis Xavier Church on Bow Bazaar Street, where Father Celeste had been sent to assist the pastor for a few days. He slept in a little room on the ground floor and nearby there was an open drain. The rats bit him four times. "The first time I woke up, but didn't see anything. The second time I noticed a red dot on my foot. The third time there were bite marks. The fourth time my foot was bathed with blood." That happened in 1986 and the infection led to gangrene. Father Celeste was operated on six times and some of his toes had to be amputated in order to save his leg. Father Celeste's room is separated from the common veranda by a folding screen and is cooled by a slow moving fan. On his bedside table are the New Testament, the Koran and a rosary. The rest of the furnishing consist of a trunk, a wash basin, and a metal ring to help him move from the bed to the bedside table, since he can no longer move around simply with the aid of a cane. He has a medal of the Blessed Virgin pinned to his shirt.

Father Celeste is an affable man, quick to respond, with merry eyes and a memory intact. He wears a white goatee and has a few remaining teeth. "I first met Mother Teresa in 1944. She was superior of the convent and head of the Bengali language section in St. Mary's School at Entally. At that time, during World War II, the school had been taken over for use as a military hospital. The Sisters in the English language section were transferred to Simia, but Mother Teresa remained in

Calcutta, in the house on Convent Road, near the mosque of Muwall Ali. She was 34 years old and appeared to be energetic and resolute, with a strong will. But physically she was weak and in danger of contracting tuberculosis. She spent all her energy for others; she ate little and slept less. If I had to describe her state at that time, I would have to use the word 'happy.' Yes, she was a woman who was absolutely, totally happy.

"Against my own wishes, I had become the chaplain for the Sisters of Loreto. I had come to Calcutta in 1938 to engage in dialogue with the Muslims. As a professor of Scriptural Exegesis, with a specialization in the Muslim world, I had been in Arabia, Syria, Iraq and Palestine, and I had lived in the desert with the Bedouin. Then I was transferred to India to study the language of the Muslims in India.

"One day Father Richier, the Rector of the Jesuit University, sent for me and asked: 'Do you want to celebrate Mass and hear confessions at the convent of the Sisters of Loreto?'

"'No, Father, I replied. You have brought me to Calcutta to start a dialogue with the Muslims, not with Sisters.'

"The Rector laughed and told me to think it over. I did not have to think very long. I was leaving the Rector's room and already had my hat on my head and my hand on the doorknob. On an impulse I turned around. 'I have thought it over; I accept.'

"And so, on July 11, 1944, I was at Convent Road. I met Mother Teresa as I was taking coffee in the parlor after Mass. I immediately liked her manner, which was at once spiritual and practical. I was impressed with her eyes, her direct and penetrating glance, and the strong lines of her face. She was very popular with the students and well liked by the Sisters. They called her the Bengali Teresa to distinguish her from Sister Marie Therese, who taught in the English language section.

"I once asked her if on entering the Sisters of Loreto she had chosen the name Teresa in honor of St. Teresa of Avila or St. Therese of Lisieux. She replied: 'The famous Teresa is not for me; the lesser known is better.'

"At the end of World War II, the Sisters were able to return to Entally and their own property. The first time I went there I was impressed by the beauty of the place: the pond, the ancient trees and the gardens of flowers around the convent and the school buildings. The Sisters were very happy to find that the mosquitoes, which had been the only flaw in that paradise, were gone. The doctors in the military hospital had sprayed the grounds with DDT.

"Mother Teresa was now no longer superior. It was a blessing for her because she no longer had to attend meetings and discussions for making important decisions. By that time she had contracted tuberculosis and the doctor had ordered her to rest in bed for at least three hours each afternoon and especially to slow down the rhythm of her daily work. That was the only time I ever saw tears in Mother Teresa's eyes. The only time. Later on she would experience the tremendous loneliness of poverty; she would see some of her beloved Sisters die; she would suffer hardships and humiliations; but I never saw her weep.

"In order to cure her lungs of the disease, the doctor sent her to breathe the pure air of Darjeeling in the convent of the Sisters of Loreto at the foot of the Himalayas. It was during the night of that journey to Darjeeling — September 10, 1946 — that she received her inspiration. I do not know if she was alone at the time; I never asked her. I do know that she found herself immersed in the Gospel-like crowd of the wretchedly poor, the crippled, the blind and the lepers. The physical contact with that suffering humanity, previously seen only from a distance, must have moved her greatly. It was a clear call which she later described as 'a vocation within a vocation.' She would work for the poorest of the poor, not in some large institution such as a hospital or hospice, but living like one of them in their very own environment.

"This physical contact, this 'being in their midst,' seems to me to be the great novelty of the religious institute founded by

Mother Teresa. To the three traditional vows of poverty, chastity and obedience, they add a fourth: the vow of charity. The Congregation of the Missionaries of Charity rests on two pillars: Jesus incarnate in the Eucharist and Jesus incarnate in the poor.

"At Darjeeling Mother Teresa had an opportunity to make the retreat preached by Father Peter Fannon, a Belgian Jesuit. Later, Father Fannon told me that Mother Teresa seemed to be very calm during the days of retreat, as if lost in meditation. He was very impressed by the intensity of her prayer.

"When Mother returned to Calcutta, she did not say anything to me for the moment. But one day when I was leaving Entally on my bicycle, I saw her hastening toward me. She signaled me to stop, waving a stack of loose sheets. I turned back: 'What are those sheets, Mother?'

"She answered with a touch of humor: 'I don't know. You will have to tell me.'

"I returned home and laid the pages on a writing table near a statue of the Blessed Mother that she had given to me for Christmas. I didn't have time to read them then, but when I read them the next day, I was startled. She had written down everything in the manner of a diary: her impressions of the poor, her inspiration, her decision to leave the Sisters of Loreto to work in the streets, and her intention to found a religious institute that would be dedicated exclusively to the poor. That bundle of handwritten pages contained in a nutshell her entire future, outlined with great clarity. The cry of the poor had reached her. She could no longer stand aloof."

* * * * *

The first advice given to Mother Teresa by her spiritual director was not to act hastily. "She was anxious to start, but I suggested that she should be patient and in the meantime pray. It was unnecessary advice because I saw that she was steeped in prayer. She did wait patiently, and in the meantime I consulted with the archbishop of Calcutta, Ferdinand Perier. He was a practical man of common sense who had become a Jesuit after having worked in a bank in his native city of Antwerp.

"'What story is this?' he exclaimed when I told him about the Albanian Sister who wanted to leave her community in order to dedicate herself to the poorest of the poor.

"I explained everything to him, and his response was a very prudent one: 'This is a very serious decision. I think she should ask for secularization. Tell her to wait for a year and during that time to be calm and to pray.'

"I relayed this message to Mother Teresa and she accepted the archbishop's decision. One morning I did not see her at Mass. I was told that she had gone to Asansol, where the Sisters of Loreto have a convent and a school. Was this some sort of punishment? No, no; no one knew of her project except myself and the archbishop.

"Mother Teresa wrote me many letters during that period. She was happy; she took care of the garden, replenished the flowers at the grotto of Our Lady of Lourdes, taught the students in the school at Asansol, and worked in the convent kitchen. The cool, dry climate of that place restored her health and gave her the strength to confront what awaited her. She had abandoned herself completely to the will of God.

"Six months later she returned to Calcutta. At that time Archbishop Perier became seriously ill. He was already advanced in years — he was in his seventies — but he lived to be 92 and died in 1968. After she arrived in Calcutta, Mother Teresa was anxious to start her new project and she wrote to the archbishop: 'Your recovery will be the sign that I can begin my work with the poor. Please, Your Grace, get well soon.'

"The archbishop did recover, and the year of waiting that he had imposed was over. He gave Mother Teresa permission to communicate her project to Mother Gertrude, the Superior General of the Sisters of Loreto in Ireland. Mother Gertrude's reply arrived on February 2, 1948, and it began with these words: "'My dear Teresa: Your project seems to me to be a clear manifestation of the will of God. I give you permission to write to Rome'."

CONVICTION

Mother Teresa's letter left Calcutta on February 7, 1948, and arrived in Rome fifteen days later. It was addressed to the Cardinal Prefect of the Congregation for Religious. At that time the Cardinal Prefect was Luigi Lavitrano and the offices of the Congregation were located in the Piazza San Calisto in the Trastevere section of Rome. One of the secretaries at the Congregation immediately removed the Indian stamps from the letter for his collection. Then he opened the letter and read the three pages with the heading "Sisters of Loreto." Next he opened a new file to be added to the thousands that already filled the shelves of the archive. "Another discontented Sister," he may have thought. He picked up a yellow index card and wrote: *Pratica 3630/48 — Diocesi di Calcutta*, and underneath: *Dame Inglese*. Later on, when the Sister became a well-known personage throughout the world, someone added with a pen: *Mother Teresa*. I received permission from the Vatican to see that file and I read the letter. It consists of three handwritten pages, in clear, large penmanship. The letter states that Sister Teresa Bojaxhiu, teacher in St. Mary's High School in Calcutta, presents her request to the Cardinal Prefect of the Congregation for Religious.

"Your Eminence: With the permission of my Mother General, I humbly ask permission to begin a life very different from that which I have lived in the convent until now, to dedicate my life to the poor in total service, following in the footsteps of St.

Francis of Assisi. Since September, 1946, God has been calling me to this. To do this work in a spirit of prayer and sacrifice, it is necessary to be close to the poor on the streets and to become poor as they are, to see Christ in every poor person. I have expressed my desire to my bishop and to my spiritual director. I have waited for a long time in order to know what has inspired me and whether this call is properly motivated. After prayer and counsel, I know that this is my vocation.

"I ask permission to serve the poor of India by living as they do. For that reason it is impossible for me to remain in the religious institute that I entered in October, 1928, and where I made my first vows.

"In all sincerity I confess that I do not possess any specific merit. To me it is a mystery that God should give me this call. In all the years that I have spent in this institute I have been happy and full of joy. Therefore, it is painful for me to leave the Sisters of Loreto, but I must take this step in the name of God, who asks of me a radical change of life. I want to do his will at any cost and gather around me souls who are disposed for this same service of seeking out the poor. There are millions of poor people here in India who live in the most abominable conditions, far removed from the grace of God and of Christ. I am a simple Sister and I don't know how to express myself well, but I ask your help to be able to be obedient to my call."

* * * * *

Mother Teresa loves to quote a proverb made famous by The Christophers: "It's better to light a candle than to curse the darkness." She lit her candle on the train to Darjeeling on September 10, 1946. She was on one of those stifling hot Indian trains, jammed with people up to the ceiling and crushed together in the stench of the passageways. Seated on a bench in third class in the midst of foul-smelling bodies and bent over the pages of her pocket-book Gospel, she must have asked: "Why,

Lord, they and not I?" St. Francis received his inspiration at Verna; that train was Mother Teresa's Verna.

She had made her decision even before she arrived at Darjeeling. She would ask permission of her superior and the archbishop of Calcutta to leave the convent and go out into the streets to seek out the poorest of the poor. The letter to the Cardinal Prefect of the Congregation for Religious was the first step.

Mother Teresa does not willingly speak about herself. One has to find the right moment and a favorable situation to get her to break her silence. It was a journalist who found the right moment and the situation to convince Mother Teresa to discuss her "vocation within a vocation." It happened in 1970 in a very significant situation; indeed, once again on the train to Darjeeling. The journalist was Desmond Doig, the editor of *The Calcutta Statesman*. Mother Teresa, Desmond Doig and two photographers, Teki and Kalyan Singh, were going to Darjeeling to perform a service for the Missionaries of Charity. The right moment arrived shortly after the train left the Howrah Station and was passing through the groves of mango orchards and palm trees of Bengal. Seated next to the window, Mother Teresa took out of her coarse cloth shopping bag a worn book entitled *Seeds of the Desert* by Charles de Foucauld. She opened it at a marker, read to the bottom of the page, and then showed Desmond Doig a passage on "the necessity of absolute dedication to the service of God." This was the moment that Desmond Doig had been waiting for, and he describes the incident in his book, *Mother Teresa: Her People and Her Work.*

> Was it true, I asked her, that it was on a train journey like this that God had revealed to her his wish that she should serve him and find him amongst life's derelicts?
>
> She nodded, but I knew from experience that she was loathe to talk about herself. Yet here I was sitting next to someone to whom God had personally spoken, and I wanted to know about the awesome

majesty of such an experience. So I persisted. "Mother, how did you know? Were you not for a second in doubt? After all, Christ himself had moments of doubt. In Gethsemane."

"No, Jesus never doubted. It was only for a moment that he felt unsure. That was as a human being. That was natural. The moment you accept, the moment you surrender yourself, that's the conviction. But it may mean death to you, eh? The conviction comes the moment you surrender yourself. Then there is no doubt. The moment Jesus said: 'Father, I am at your disposal, thy will be done,' he had accepted. That was his agony. He felt all the things you and I would feel as human beings. That's why he was like unto us in all things, except sin."

"But what if uncertainty remains?"

"That's the time to go on your knees, eh? ... In that prayer God cannot deceive you because that prayer comes from within you. That is the time you want him most. Once you have got God within you, that's for life. There is no doubt. You can have other doubts, eh? But that particular one will never come again... No, I have never doubted.... But I'm convinced that it is he and not I. That it is his work, and not mine. I am only at his disposal. Without him I can do nothing. But even God could do nothing for someone already full. You have to be completely empty to let him in, to do what he wills. That's the most beautiful part of God, eh? Being almighty, and yet not forcing himself on anyone."

"But Mother, you surely have to use your initiative?"

"Of course. You have to do it as if everything depends on you — but leave the rest to God."

GOD'S VAGABOND

The day after my first interview with Father Celeste van Exem I went back to see him. When he was unable to sleep during the night, he used the time to jot down some points and some names. He wanted to put some order in the recollections that he would present to me. From the courtyard of the university I could hear the shouts of the students who were playing soccer. Father van Exem began speaking:

"On the first Sunday of August in 1948 I was ready to consign to Mother Teresa the decree of exclaustration that had been granted by Pope Pius XII. At that time the power to grant such a decree was reserved exclusively to the Holy See. Exclaustration carried with it a dispensation from certain aspects of the vows and from all religious observances that are incompatible with the new condition of life. Practically speaking, Mother Teresa was still a Sister, but she could leave the convent and live alone, in accordance with the regulations of the archbishop. It meant that the archbishop had become her superior.

"When I delivered the decree, there was a certain amount of turmoil among the Sisters of Loreto. I remember three distinct reactions. Mother Teresa made no comment; the only thing she asked was: 'Now can I go into the slums?' But the superior, Mother de Cenacle, reacted with tears: 'What have I done wrong? Teresa is my right hand; I cannot cut off my right hand!'

I tried to pacify her: 'Either this is the will of God or it is not the will of God. If it is God's will, we must accept it. If it is not God's will, we shall soon see Mother Teresa back in the convent.' The superior then stopped weeping.

"The reaction of the Provincial, Mother Columba, seemed more moderate. She put the following notice on the bulletin board: 'Dear Sisters: Teresa is leaving the convent. Do not praise. Do not criticize. Pray.' They were the right words.

"Mother Teresa always knew what she wanted. I don't know anyone who is more prompt in making a decision and then putting it into practice at once. The following day she went to the market and bought two saris of white cotton with a blue border; they were the kind worn by the poor people in India. There are also saris with a red border, but Mother Teresa chose blue in honor of the Blessed Virgin.

"We had a little ceremony in the chapel. Mother Teresa prayed, Mother de Cenacle wept again, and I blessed the saris. Then Mother Teresa left for Patna, an all-night journey by train from Calcutta. She went to the Holy Family Hospital conducted by the American Medical Missionaries in order to get some experience in nursing, about which she knew nothing. She went all alone, after taking off the habit of the Sisters of Loreto and putting on the sari. All she had was her train ticket and five rupees. The students came to bid her farewell and were surprised to see their former teacher dressed in a sari. They had always seen her in the black habit of the Sisters of Loreto."

That evening in August Mother Teresa had asked not to be accompanied to the train for Patna, nor did her new condition of poverty permit her to take a taxi or a rickshaw. She headed for the train station on foot, carrying her rosary, her train ticket and five rupees. She was truly God's vagabond and she had risked everything to answer her call. Later, she wrote: "I walked until I could walk no farther. I now understood better what exhaustion the poor must experience, always in search of everything. The memory of the tranquillity I enjoyed in the convent was a temptation for me. I prayed: 'No, I shall not turn back. My house is the house of the poor'."

* * * * *

At this point Father van Exem consulted his notes; he wanted to be sure of not confusing the dates: "The following day, August 19, 1948, Mother Teresa was at Patna, ready to begin her courses of instruction on nursing. During the following weeks she wrote to me several times. She was quickly learning from the American Medical Missionaries and was getting practice in the hospital wards, gaining confidence in caring for the sick and administering medicine. In one of her last letters from Patna she said that she felt that she was now ready to return to Calcutta and begin her work among the poor.

"Once again I had to restrain her, and since I had to go to that area in September to preach a retreat, I made a detour in order to visit her. There was a group of nurses in front of the hospital and I asked where I could find Mother Teresa. A voice spoke up: 'Father, Father, here I am.' I had not recognized her because I was not used to seeing her in the sari.

"She began to insist: 'I am ready; I am able to administer medicines and give injections.' I spoke with the superior, Sister Stephanie, a very competent American, and with the head of the hospital, Sister Elise, who was Dutch. They both testified that Mother Teresa had been an exceptional student, and in order to reassure me, they added that she would not be giving medical care by herself because there would be doctors and nurses nearby to assist her. I trusted their professional competence because the American Medical Missionaries, founded by Mother Anna Dengel, had much experience and an excellent reputation. They conducted a famous hospital at Delhi and were highly regarded."

* * * * *

This particular evening Father van Exem was tired; he said that his legs felt as heavy as rocks. The heat today has reached 106 degrees Fahrenheit in the shade. There are days when Calcutta is intolerably oppressive because of the intense heat, the air pollution, the dust and the overcast skies. Then one desperately yearns to see white clouds floating in the blue sky and to feel on one's face the cool breezes coming down from the hills. At Ypres, in Father van Exem's native land of Belgium, there are green fields and a countryside covered with flowers. But it was also at Ypres that poison gas was used for the first time by the Germans in the First World War. Father van Exem recalled those days when he saw soldiers from the trenches come to his home and beg for a glass of water. Their lungs had been burned by the mustard gas. Later he became a Jesuit and a missionary and has travelled all over the world, but he has never forgotten those scenes.

"I have had a long and happy life. Life, after all, is a matter of choice, and I have chosen well. If I were to do it all over again, I would do the same."

"Even including the rats, Father van Exem?"

"The rats are incidental; it could have been much worse. They have confined me to bed with gangrene, but I am not alone. Formerly it was I who went to visit others; now it is the others who visit me. But that's all right. Mother Teresa comes to see me, and when she has no time, she writes to me, as she used to do. She has always written to me frequently."

"What will you do with all the letters? Will you publish them?"

"Oh, no! They are letters of conscience, very personal. I shall not leave them in any archive; I shall destroy them before I die. This is also Mother's wish."

Father van Exem recalled that Archbishop Perier had asked Mother Teresa to write the history of her Congregation from its beginning. Each evening, after a day of exhausting labor, Mother Teresa worked on a diary that recorded the significant events that occurred to her and her Sisters. In a short time, however, she realized that she could not continue the work. Depriving herself of much-needed sleep, she was soon fully occupied with answering letters from women who wanted to become Missionaries of Charity, from persons who sought her help, and from people who sent contributions for the work. Consequently, the diary that records the history of the early years of the Missionaries of Charity remains unfinished. Mother Teresa gave it to Father van Exem, who cherished it for many years, until she asked him to return it. She said that she was going to destroy it. We can imagine that she had written in the laconic style that was typical of her manner of speaking. Perhaps she had also described incommunicable experiences that only a mystical heart would receive.

IN CREEK LANE

L ower Circle Road is a great highway of six lanes, with two tracks in the center for the streetcars. The din of the heavy traffic is punctuated by the constant blowing of horns. Creek Lane crosses Lower Circle Road, which is a narrow, quiet street, like a calm tributary branching off from a turbulent river. It is protected from the bustle of heavy traffic because of its narrowness; nothing larger than a rickshaw travels on it. The houses along this street still show traces of the sumptuousness that was characteristic of Calcutta when it was known as "the city of palaces." It was the imperial capital until 1912.

Time, monsoons and neglect have caused the cornices of the buildings to crumble, have worn down the ornamentation on the stone window frames, and have corroded the gates and the street lamps. But there is still a touch of beauty in the emaciated bougainvillea that climbs toward the spire of the temple in honor of the god Siva. Creek Lane is a time-worn lady, but it still has some traces of its former splendor.

Curiously, on this very street which once housed the wealthy bourgeoisie, Mother Teresa found a home after leaving the Sisters of Loreto. It was in a house that belonged to the Gomes family.

"Yes, we provided the first house for Mother Teresa when she left Entally," said Michael Gomes, 83 years old. Like many well-to-do Indians, he does not appear so. He is short and thin and wears glasses. He has few lines on his dark-complexioned face, which emerges from a white, short-sleeved shirt. I had seen him serving Mass at the Motherhouse of the Missionaries of Charity. I was struck by the amiability that seemed to emanate from a hidden smile and the modest manner in which he moved about the altar in his bare feet.

Mother Teresa knows that I am writing about him; she does all she can to get me to talk about "her people." Whenever I ask her about the past, she always says: "My story is not important." But she respects the work of others, even the probing work of a journalist. She once suggested with a touch of affection: "Speak with Mr. Gomes, He remembers many things about me."

Mr. Gomes was very available. "Come whenever you want. I am free every day after nine o'clock. I am on pension now and I do not have many engagements. At dawn I arrive at the Motherhouse to serve Mass, and on the way back home I stop at the market to do my shopping. My wife seldom leaves the house. I live at Number 14 on Creek Lane, a little narrow street that is not well known. Tell the taxi driver that it is near the hospital Nilratan Sarkar."

There is an arched entrance at Number 14 Creek Lane. Beyond the front gate there is a two-story wooden stairway, and from the brightly lighted veranda one enters a dimly lighted room with many doors. On the walls there are family photos and oil paintings of Mahatma Gandhi, Pandit Nehru and Mother Teresa, evidently favorite persons. Everything is neatly arranged and polished. The Gomes family keeps out the heat, odors and humidity of Calcutta by keeping the Venetian blinds lowered and by daily cleaning.

"My grandfather built this house. He worked as a building contractor and he bought and sold houses. He was a very successful business man. My family is descended from Portuguese who were merchants in India 400 years ago. We are

Catholics. My father worked in the central post office. He was a very religious man. Before going to work he attended Mass every morning at the parish church of Our Lady of Sorrows. My mother always went with him."

* * * * *

In a photo of the family, taken in 1920, Mr. Gomes' parents, Augustus and Sabina, are elegantly dressed in a mixture of Indian and European fashion. Augustus wears glasses and a mustache and is dressed in a suit coat, stiff collar and tie. Sabina is elegantly and modestly garbed in a sari, with her long hair falling loosely over her shoulders. Around them are their nine children, with very dark eyes — four boys in European shirts and trousers and five girls dressed in Bengali style. In another photo, taken in 1938, Michael Gomes and his wife Agnes are dressed in similar fashion — Michael in a suit coat and Agnes in a sari.

"That was the year we made a trip to Italy. We visited the Sistine chapel in Rome. My wife wore a green sari with a gold border, and everybody stared at her with great curiosity."

Michael and Agnes now live alone in this large house and they use the rooms facing the front entrance. In the bedrooms there is a canopy over the beds as well as mosquito netting; in the study there is a large collection of books in Bengali and in English; the parlor and the dining room are furnished with colonial style furniture made of teakwood. Everything bespeaks a comfortable life and a high social class. Michael Gomes had been a high ranking official, holding various positions in government administration, not the least being that of Director of Information Service for the State of Bengal. He has been pensioned for the last 20 years.

Their only daughter, Mabel Sophia, moved to the United States with her husband, a chemical engineer, and their three children. When she was seven years old, Mabel Sophia was the little instrument used by God to obtain the first lodging for Mother Teresa. That was in February, 1949.

* * * * *

"The upper floor was once occupied by two of my brothers. One was a deputy in the National Assembly and the other was a director in the post office. When the Indian Empire was divided in 1947 and Bengal was partitioned into two States, my two brothers went to East Pakistan. The archbishop of Calcutta had advised them to make that transfer for two reasons. First, he thought that since they were Catholics and held important positions, they might be exposed to persecution. Secondly, their presence in Pakistan would be helpful to the little community of Catholics in that area. After they left, the upper floor remained vacant.

"At the end of 1948 our mother, who was already advanced in years, became ill. One of my other brothers, Alfred, asked the parish priest, Father Celeste van Exem, to administer the last sacraments to her. Father van Exem arrived, gave Communion to my mother, and then stayed for a while to talk with us. It was evident that he had something important to request of us.

"'Do you know Mother Teresa?,' he asked. 'She is a Sister of Loreto who has left the convent in order to dedicate herself to the service of the poor. She has just returned from Patna, where she was studying nursing in the hospital of the American Sisters. For the moment she is staying with the Little Sisters of the Poor, but she considers that only a temporary situation. She has to be free in order to do the work she has in mind. She needs a permanent lodging.'

"Alfred and I did not have time to respond because my daughter immediately blurted out: 'Papa, why don't you give her the upper floor?'

"We two brothers discussed the possibility and finally

decided to do so. The upper floor was empty, with the furniture in place. Father van Exem said that one room would be sufficient. Obviously, we did not ask her to pay any rent.

"Mother Teresa arrived here on a day in February in 1949. She was alone and was dressed in a sari, which was most unusual for a nun from the West. Under her arm she carried a black shopping bag of coarse cloth, containing all her belongings. I told her that she could use any furniture she needed, but she replied that she would not need any. She was content with a cot for sleeping, a packing box for a desk, and some smaller boxes to serve as chairs.

"Her first project was a school, and it is not by chance that she had been a teacher for almost twenty years. She went to Moti Jihl, the poor people's quarter adjacent to the wall of the school and convent at Entally. She gathered some children together in an empty space surrounded by the thatched huts of the poor. There were no desks, no blackboard, no chalk. With the help of a man who was lounging nearby, she cleared the ground of grass and debris, and using a stick, she traced the letters of the Bengali alphabet on the ground. She ended the lesson by reciting a poem and concluded with a prayer.

"The next day someone brought her a table and a stool. Later she was able to rent a hut for five rupees a month and there she put her first sick people. I helped her to get medicine from a friend of mine who was an official in the Department of Health. Yes, Mother Teresa gets what she wants, and when she doesn't, she is content nevertheless. She would then say: 'Evidently it was not God's will'."

At that moment Agnes, the wife of Michael Gomes, entered the parlor with a tea tray. Her tranquil face still bears the traces of former beauty. She does not speak English, so she asks in Bengali if she may stay with us and listen to the account, which she must have heard so many times before. Guessing at what her husband was saying in English, she nodded in assent. Mr. Gomes speaks of Mother Teresa with reverence and affection. He also, like his daughter Mabel Sophia, feels that he is an instrument in God's plan.

"Mother was 39 years old when she came here. Now she has arthritis, but then she was erect, strong and indefatigable. She was full of life and joy. Every evening, after spending the day on the streets, begging for charity so that she could carry food to the families in the slums of Moti Jihl, she would return here, and after an hour in prayer, she would wash the stairs, scrubbing the wooden steps with soap and water. As tired as she was after her day's work, she still had the strength to wash two flights of stairs. She did this to repay us for our hospitality, and she would not stop. My wife told her not to do it, but Mother Teresa paid no attention. She has always been obstinate.

"Sometimes my wife would take her some food, but the next day she always found the plate untouched. A bowl of rice and some vegetables were enough for Mother Teresa. She would prepare it in the evening, in the little pan that she had brought with her. I don't know how she could be on her feet all day, working, with the little nourishment that she took. When my wife would scold her, she would say with a smile that the poor have less to eat than she does."

Agnes Gomes nods her head in agreement and Michael Gomes is deeply moved by this remembrance. He hesitates for a moment, as if searching for the right words.

"Have you been to Entally? Have you seen that beautiful place — the marvelous chapel, the well-organized school, the comfortable convent? Then you can understand what I am about to tell you. The biographers of Mother Teresa have stated that she received some kind of illumination concerning the poor during that train ride on September 10, 1946. I don't know... I think that even before that, Mother Teresa agonized over the condition of the poor. From the window of her room on the first floor of the convent she could see the street and how the people lived there — cooking their meals and sleeping on the sidewalk, and the naked children running around in the filth of the city street. I believe that for a long time she had prayed and meditated until she was ready to make her great decision."

* * * * *

Mother Teresa did not remain alone for very long in the Gomes home. Michael remembers the first girls who were attracted to her ideal and followed her. The very first one was Subashini Das, a very small girl with shining eyes. As a religious she took Mother Teresa's baptismal name, Agnes. Today it is rumored among the Missionaries of Charity that she will be the next Mother General of the Congregation.

Subashini had been a student of Mother Teresa in St. Mary's High School at Entally. In one of the rare interviews that Subashini granted — and I really don't know how that happened, because she is very reserved — she said: "Besides English and geography, Mother Teresa taught us religion, and she did so in such a way that everything became vividly clear before our eyes. Through her words the love of Jesus and the remembrance of his sacrifice was branded on the soul. We understood the beauty of sacrificing ourselves in turn for him."

The second girl to join Mother Teresa was Magdalen Gomes, who became Sister Gertrude in religion. Then other former students and girls who learned about the work of "the Sister in the sari" became members without any kind of persuasion. As Mahatma Gandhi has said: "A rose does not need to preach. Its fragrance is its sermon." Or, as St. Clare said of St. Francis of Assisi: "He was silent, but his reputation cried out."

One after another, the future Missionaries of Charity knocked at the door of Number 14, Creek Lane. A new religious institute is being born, but as yet no one knows what it will be. Although they had no written rule of life, the first members lived like religious, all garbed in the same type of sari and motivated by "the beauty of sacrificing themselves for him." All they knew was that the new religious institute would sooner or later be approved, and in the meantime they lived under obedience to Archbishop Perier of Calcutta.

* * * * *

With the arrival of the new recruits, the wooden stairway of the Gomes house resounded with the footsteps of the young women. "At dawn they swarmed into Creek Lane, and the street was made cheerful by the presence of those young women dressed in white saris. They would return home in the evening and spend an hour absorbed in silent prayer and meditation. After that, we would hear singing and laughter as they recreated together. Sometimes Mother Teresa would bring the girls down to the yard for recreation and games.... On holidays, when the whole city was celebrating, Mother Teresa did not have the money to buy the traditional sweets, but she always managed to get a bag of *chinabadam*, a mixture of roasted nuts. We could hear them sing, clapping their hands, and always there was the cry 'Mother! Mother!' She was the focal point in everything. It seemed as if this old house had returned to the times when we, who were nine brothers and sisters, made a lot of noise with our games as children.

"Once Cardinal Spellman of New York visited Calcutta and Archbishop Perier brought him here. Mother Teresa showed him the large room in which the Sisters lived. 'This is our refectory, Your Eminence.'

"'And the dormitory?' he asked.

"'It is here. We move the tables and set up the cots.'

"'The chapel?'

"'It is also here, Your Eminence.'" And Mother showed him the altar behind the screen. The cardinal laughed, and Mother Teresa with him. She is always ready to laugh, although now less frequently because she is preoccupied with many responsibilities.

"Only once did I see Mother Teresa cry, and that was when

one of the Sisters died. She had been bitten by a stray dog and had contracted rabies. Mother spoke to me through her tears: 'She is here in the bed, suffering convulsions from the sickness, but she seems concerned only with not showing herself and constantly pulling on the sari to make it reach down to her ankles'."

* * * * *

There are three dormers protruding from the roof of the Gomes house which Mother Teresa had converted into shower rooms. From up there, Creek Lane looks like a deep and narrow canyon, but looking beyond that, one can see all of Calcutta with its splendors and its horrors. Michael Gomes pointed out to me the bell towers of churches, the minarets of mosques, the spires of the Hindu temples, the vast expanse of slums, the steel towers of the Howrah Bridge, over which a million persons pass each day. Lower down on the roof flocks of crows are flying around, curious at our presence.

"In Bengali we call them *kak*," said Michael, "because that is their cry all day long: kak, kak, kak."

We then go down into the house in search of a cool spot. The sun is so bright that it hurts the eyes and the intensity of its heat is felt even on the veranda.

"Mother Teresa stayed with us a little less than two years. The number of Sisters had increased to 28 and there was no longer enough room for so many. Father van Exem found a new residence for them not far from here, on Lower Circle Road. The owner was a Muslim named Doctor Islam. He was a judge and a very pious man. He asked Father van Exem: 'What makes you think that I want to sell? My wife and I have never spoken of it.'

"The house was very big because Dr. Islam had built it so that he could retire there with his family and servants when he would be pensioned. After hearing Father van Exem's request, he asked Father to be patient for a moment while he went to pray

47

in the mosque at Muwall Ali. When he returned, he told Father that he had decided to sell the house to Mother Teresa. 'I have received this house from God,' he said, 'and I return it to God.' Mother Teresa did not have the money to pay for it, so Archbishop Perier helped her."

On October 7, 1950, the new Congregation of the Missionaries of Charity was approved and established in Calcutta. Shortly thereafter Mother Teresa and her Sisters moved to Number 54/A on Lower Circle Road. The house was a large edifice of three stories, with an internal courtyard. It now became the Motherhouse of the Missionaries of Charity, the center of all Mother Teresa's apostolic works. Michael Gomes continued to help Mother with his advice and his contacts with influential officials.

* * * * *

Lunch is now ready. Agnes Gomes has prepared *mulligatani* (lentil soup flavored with curry), lightly cooked vegetables and boiled rice. But Michael lets his food get cold, ignoring the disapproving glances of his wife. He has so many memories that crowd into his mind.

"One day Mother Teresa told me that the government of Bengali was willing to give her 33 rupees for every infant she cared for. I advised her to think it over before accepting the offer. As a civil servant, I knew how demanding the bureaucracy can be. It would demand financial reports, a list of receipts, the keeping of books, a board of controllers — in a word, everything that the law requires of those who handle public funds. Mother did not seem to be concerned about that. 'And so?' she replied. 'We can entrust it to a small committee of friends and you will help me with the accounts.' As usual, she was quick to make a decision and she was very optimistic. I said nothing more.

"Some time later, she told me that on returning from the government offices, she began to sing to herself on the streetcar.

I asked her why she was so happy. 'Because I had gone to the officials to tell them that I renounce the public funding. You were right; too much paper work, too many regulations and too much trouble. Moreover, they require that I spend 33 rupees for each child, but I am now spending only 17 rupees.'

"That's the way Mother Teresa is — as free and independent as the air. She doesn't like regulations. Once a functionary sent the superior of the house in Delhi a written order to turn over to the chauffeur four of the blankets that had just arrived in a shipment from a foreign country. Mother Teresa happened to be present at the time and she took the paper and wrote on the reverse side in large letters: 'The blankets are for the poor.' Yes, she is a resolute and forceful woman."

For Michael Gomes it was a source of affectionate pride that from the very beginning he had helped that little woman who is now the personification of the Gospel teaching.

"Even now, though more than 80 years old, she makes all the decisions. No one can push her aside. I don't know where she gets such energy; or rather, I do know very well. She has her feet on the ground and her heart above the clouds. She lives on the level of the transcendental, and yet she has a genius for practical matters. I once told her that, and she explained that it was through prayer that she was able to strike the proper balance between earth and heaven.

"One evening we were at table in the Motherhouse, where I sometimes stop to eat, and Mother Teresa had not yet returned home. The Sisters and I began to be a bit worried. Then she arrived in a truck, seated on sacks of flour. There she was, up there, perched on top of the shipment, praying the rosary. I gently reprimanded her — sometimes she permits me to do so. I told her that she could have sent one of the Sisters to do that task. She replied that the authorities are always kinder to her and that it was better to handle that job in person so that no one would steal anything."

I myself was present at a similar incident. It happened in

Tirana, Albania, on the vigil of Easter in 1991. Mother Teresa had just received a shipment of sacks of rice from Caritas, but the truck was too big to enter the Ali Pasha quarter where she had recently opened a house. With the help of some officials from the Italian Embassy, a plan was worked out: the huge truck could be parked in front of the Embassy and a smaller truck would shuttle back and forth with the bags of rice. Mother Teresa supervised the transfer to the smaller truck and then climbed up on top to make sure that nothing would disappear en route to the house.

At eleven o'clock at night the transfer of the shipment was still unfinished, and some of the volunteers went home. The policeman on guard at the Embassy was still at his post, so Mother Teresa approached him and held out to him a small religious medal. The policeman looked at the medal, somewhat puzzled, not knowing what to do. Mother then placed the medal in the pocket over his heart and said something to him. Then the policeman laid his gun on the ground and proceeded to help unload the sacks of rice. Mother Teresa smiled as she bent over to help him. I intervened, saying: "Mother, you shouldn't exert yourself that way. Then I added somewhat rudely: "at your age." She turned her head to one side, looked me up and down, and said with a self-satisfied smile: "And I also have a pacemaker."

* * * * *

On October 7, 1975, the Missionaries of Charity celebrated the twenty-fifth anniversary of their foundation. The church was overflowing with people at the jubilee ceremony. Mother Teresa's oldest friends, who had helped her from the beginning, were gathered around her: Father Julian Henry, Father Celeste van Exem, Sister Agnes, Sister Gertrude.... The honor of serving the Mass, which was celebrated by Archbishop Picachy of Calcutta and about 20 concelebrants, was reserved for the layman who had provided Mother Teresa with her first residence: Michael Gomes. As usual, Michael moved about the altar with humble reverence and with bare feet. Every once in a while he glanced with deep feeling at the first pew, where his wife Agnes and his daughter Mabel Sophia, with her three children, were seated.

In bidding me farewell at the door, Michael Gomes said: "I don't ask myself what Mother Teresa has done for India and for all of humanity. I say only that she has followed an inspiration from on high and she has compelled us to follow it."

LIFE IS LIFE: SAVE IT

S hishu Bhavan means Children's Home, and it is located at Number 78 on Lower Circle Road, a short distance from the Motherhouse, which is Number 54/A. Life in the Motherhouse is very orderly and silent and it follows a rigid schedule. Visitors are admitted only for Mass or for some urgent need. Of the approximately 200 Sisters in residence, most of them leave the house after Mass, two by two or in groups, and hasten to their daily work. The few who remain at home bid the others farewell at the gate. Every time I observe that morning departure, which is the same in every house of the Missionaries of Charity, the words of Dante come to mind: "As sheep do when they come out of a fold, by ones and twos and threes, and the others stand timidly putting nose and eyes to earth" (*Purgatorio*, stanza 79). The Sisters hurry to catch the streetcar on Lower Circle Road or else set out on foot, walking quickly, with the customary cloth shopping bag on their arm and the rosary between their fingers. They are going in search of human rejects, obedient to the command of Mother Teresa: "Give me your hands to care for the poorest of the poor and your hearts to love them."

* * * * *

The traffic in the large cities of the West is an orderly, quiet procession when compared to the noisy confusion on Lower

Circle Road. The streetcars rumble down the center of the highway with people perched on the roof or clinging to the windows like bunches of grapes. The four lanes of the street are choked with automobiles that would be rejected even by the auto-wreckers, motor bikes that give off a deafening sound, and blocked trucks blasting their horns and emitting clouds of black smoke from their exhaust pipes. Meanwhile, the trotting men pulling rickshaws do their best to squeeze through the serpentine maze of metal and the ant-hill of pedestrians. It is the only means of transport that can make its way through the blocked traffic. I set out for Shishu Bhavan, the Children's Home, at seven o'clock, before the sun sends down its wave of humid heat on the city. Kazim, the owner of a snack shop, greets me and invites me to enter. By this time I know the shop well because I have eaten his *dalpuries*, a type of fritter or pancake, and *haluwa*, a cold soup made with curry. This morning Kazim offers me a refreshing drink made of anice. He is a Muslim and he tells me that I should visit the little blue-tiled mosque next door, but I always find it closed. Two numbers down the street is the vendor of betel. His name is Paan, and he is already at his stand, which is simply an opening about the size of a window. He is preparing the fresh merchandise for the day. With a pair of scissors he cuts off the glossy leaves of the Piper betel; then he wraps them around a stick of cinnamon, a piece of the *areca catechu* nut, and a little calcium. The result is a morsel to chew on. It costs only two rupees, a price that even the poor can afford. The benefit of this snack is that it produces a slight narcotic effect that helps poor people endure the hunger that makes the day seem endless.

* * * * *

The Motherhouse of the Missionaries of Charity, as we have said, is an oasis of tranquillity and peace; the Children's Home, on the other hand, is a whirlpool of joyful chaos. It resounds with the squalling of newborn infants, the shouts of small children playing in the courtyard, and the agitation of the pregnant girls who have been cast out by their families and are here waiting to deliver. A childless couple arrives to inquire about adopting a baby; poor people are waiting patiently in line for a bowl of rice; sick people are arriving for medication or injections. While the Motherhouse represents the contemplative aspect of the life of the Sisters, Shishu Bhavan is an illustration of their active apostolate. It serves as an emergency clinic, a center for receiving abandoned infants, a 24-hour pharmacy, a soup kitchen, an office for processing the adoption of babies, and a maternity counseling center.

There is already a line of people in front of the gate. The people who sleep on the sidewalk awake at the first light of day. Those who have blankets fold them up; those who do not, take the ragged piece of cotton cloth that covered them during the night and use it as clothing during the day. The men wrap it around their waist and the women drape it around themselves like a sari. They wash themselves at one of the numerous city fountains. Water is one of the few things that are not lacking in Calcutta, a city built on marshes, frequently visited by monsoon rains, and divided in two by the Hooghly River. The street people use their fingers as a toothbrush, a bit of earth as soap, and a bucket of water for a shower. They do all this in the open, with the drainage canals serving as latrines. Privacy is a luxury of the rich. Now the people are waiting while the rice is being cooked under a lean-to in the courtyard. It is being prepared in huge kettles placed on rocks that surround a coal fire. Sisters are stirring the rice with ladles so large that it takes two Sisters to rotate them. The line of people silently inches forward, each person holding a metal bowl, a dish, or an empty tin can. Each one receives a ladle of rice and then goes off to face a new day. A notice is posted in front of the office in the courtyard: "Interviews for adoptions between 8:30 and 11:30, except on Thursdays and Sundays."

It is not yet 8:30 and Sister Alex, the superior, has time to read the paper. She shows me an article on the first page of *The Telegraph*. It states that according to some American scientists, the smoke from the burning oil wells in Kuwait, set afire during the Gulf War, may possibly affect the cycle of monsoons on the Indian subcontinent. That would be a great calamity. Monsoons, like the goddess Kali, can bring life or death, blessing or curse. If a monsoon comes peacefully, it is of great benefit to the dried-up fields; it sustains the rice plants and prevents them from withering; it cools the scorching winds. But if a monsoon arrives with fury, it causes floods that ruin the harvest in the fields and inundate the slums in the city, causing millions of people to flee from their dilapidated hovels. Sister Alex asks me to wait for Sister Mary Peter, who is in charge of adoptions. On the wall behind Sister Alex is a poster containing one of the instructions of Mother Teresa: "I prefer that you make mistakes through kindness than that you work miracles with rudeness."

* * * * *

The use of these teaching posters is characteristic of all the houses of the Missionaries of Charity. At Shishu Bhavan, a place for desperate people in search of hope, the posters serve as a source of instruction and encouragement. One of the posters has a water-color painting of two trees: the tree of self-pity and the tree of self-realization. The first tree, painted in an ugly brown color, is dried up and without leaves. On each of its roots is painted a word: fear, resentment, distrust, hostility, guilt feelings. The poison rises from the roots to the branches, which bear the following labels: alcoholism, drug addiction, alienation, loneliness, neurosis. The second tree is healthy and covered with green leaves. Its roots are marked as follows: love, friendship, charity, pardon, trust. The life-giving sap rises to the branches, which are identified as well-being, joy, acceptance, creativity, and freedom.

Other posters contain simple, helpful counsels, for example: "The pleasure of walking"; "Walking is an exercise that doesn't require a gymnasium. It is a prescription without medicine, a control of weight without dieting, a cosmetic that is not found in a boutique, a tranquillizer without pills, a therapy without psychoanalysis, a fountain of youth that is not a fable, a vacation that costs nothing."

One entire wall in the office is a collage of photos of Mother Teresa, and on each photo there is a brief comment. In one of the photos Mother Teresa is bending over a sick person at Kalighat and the notation reads: "Love is a fruit for all seasons and is within the reach of all." Another photo shows Mother Teresa in the midst of handicapped children: "One must do God's work in his way." Yet another photo shows the Sisters in chapel: "It is impossible to engage in the direct apostolate without being a person of prayer." Finally, there is a photo of Queen Elizabeth embracing Mother Teresa, and the comment is a statement made by Jesus, without any irony intended: "What you have done to the least of my little ones, you have done to me."

* * * * *

Sister Mary Peter arrives, a short and lively Bengali. She leads me into a second courtyard that is more crowded and congested than the other one. The Sisters' saris that are hung out to dry form a curtained area in which groups of children are playing, hidden from view. They pay no attention to the young Sister who appears from time to time and scolds them for playing there. But my arrival saves the laundry; the children run to me and crowd around me, crying: "Auntie! Auntie! Take my picture!" They mimic the taking of a photo by making a circle with the thumb and forefinger and holding it up to their eyes. Meanwhile, one of the larger children plays at driving the ambulance that was donated by the makers of Fiat in India, calling to the Sister to look at him. Elsewhere, a small child with big eyes chases after two frightened chickens. Rising above the courtyard is an old villa decorated with colorful tile and mosaics portraying the theme of liberty. Formerly it was the headquarters of a political party but it was donated to Mother Teresa ten years ago. In the parlor on the ground floor there are cribs for the newborn infants, ten in each row. Some of the babies are lying motionless in a state of lethargy; others, only a few months old, have enough strength to hold out their thin arms. Many of these babies were picked up from the gutter or discovered in a pile of rubbish; others were abandoned and left in front of the police station, and the police brought them here. More than half of these infants die, either because they are premature births or are the result of a late abortion.

There is such a strong instinctual need for love in these abandoned infants that even if they are only a few months old, they will follow you with their eyes and hold out their arms to be picked up and held. However, a notice on the wall warns visitors: "Remove your shoes. Do not pick up the infants. Do not kiss them." Moving among the cribs, carrying diapers and rubber toys, are a few Missionaries of Charity and the Indian ladies who help them. Sister Mary Peter gave me this information about adoptions:

"The couples who want to adopt a baby can choose a boy or a girl. The Indians prefer a male; the Westerners prefer a female. For an Indian family, a male gives promise of later assistance to the family; for the Westerners, the female is a source of affection. Another preference of adopting couples is for the youngest and smallest infant, although in the end they are usually willing to forego that preference.

"We have had generous couples who adopted handicapped babies, but we keep the severely handicapped ones. We take care of them and some of them do make some progress. We have had some blind children and some with deformed legs who have been operated on and then let out for adoption. One can ask generosity of adopting parents, but not heroism. Still there have been some who were heroic. For example, a couple from Switzerland adopted an infant who had to have its blood changed every three months. The baby is now two years old; it is cured and is much loved. We are able to follow the baby's progress through the photos that the mother sends to us regularly.

"In 1990 we gave out 97 babies for adoption by Indian couples and 208 by European families. The procedure is simple. The request is made at one of our houses in the nation of residence of the adopting parents. That's where the process begins, and there must be a verification that the petitioners are qualified to adopt a baby. The following factors must be investigated: the health of the prospective parents, their financial situation and their ability to raise a child. The results are sent to the court for minors and in the meantime we send to the petitioners two or three photos of babies that are eligible for adoption. We also send some information about the baby: name, date of birth, and why the baby was abandoned. Usually it takes three or four months from the beginning of the process until the baby is handed over. Then it is better if the adopting parents can come to get the baby; otherwise we send the baby to them with one of our Sisters who is travelling to that place.

"A few days ago Mother and three Sisters left for Rome and they took four infants to Italian families. Two weeks ago an Italian couple who had already adopted one of our infants came back here and adopted a nine-year-old girl who had been abandoned at Darjeeling."

* * * * *

In the waiting room for adopting parents the "Hymn to Life" is posted on the wall:

> Life is an opportunity; seize it.
> Life is beauty; admire it.
> Life is a dream; realize it.
> Life is a duty; fulfill it.
> Life is a game; play it.

Life is a mystery; know it.
Life is a promise; keep it.
Life is sorrow; surmount it.
Life is a song; sing it.
Life is a struggle; fight it.
Life is an adventure; challenge it.

I don't know who composed this hymn to life; it seems to come out of the Anglo-saxon culture, which is greatly attracted to this style of writing. Mother Teresa has added to the list in her own hand:

Life is life; save it.

* * * * *

Mother Teresa is a specialist in human suffering and misery. I believe that no other person has ever seen as much horror and suffering as she has. In spite of this, Mother Teresa remains a lover of life. When they gave her the Nobel Peace Prize in 1979, she gave what was for her an unusually long speech, and the central part of her message was dedicated to the defense of life.

"We combat abortion with adoption. We have saved thousands of lives. We circulate this message in hospitals, clinics and police stations: 'Please, do not kill the infant before it is born. Entrust it to us.' As a result, every hour of the day and night there is always somebody — as you know, there are many unmarried mothers among us — to whom we can say: 'Come, we will take care of you; we will hold the baby that will be born of you; we will give it a family.' And we have an enormous number of requests from couples that have no children. This is a blessing of the Lord for us." The poet, Rabindranath Tagore, the sweet singer of Bengal, has written: "Every baby that is born/ brings with it the hope/ that God is no longer/ disappointed with man."

LEPROSY'S CHILDREN

itagarh, on the northern periphery of Calcutta, is an unclean world enclosed within a high wall; there the most untouchable of the untouchables are confined. It is a colony of 2,000 lepers. In the narrow lanes that skirt a sea of mud, amid the stench of the sewers and the attacks of clouds of insects, the aged lepers lie on fiber mats, their hands and feet bound in rags. Here and there an attentive grandchild waves a fan back and forth over the face of a grandparent. On the threshold of the hut the women cook rice over a fire made from dried cow dung. The men occupy themselves with little tasks such as collecting nails from a pile of metal scraps. The children romp around, completely naked, joyful even in the midst of such misery and filth. Their little bodies are as yet unmarked by the symptoms of leprosy that eats away the fingers, toes and noses of their elders and makes their skin resemble that of an armadillo.

* * * * *

Each morning John Raju leaves the leper colony. With the aid of crutches he skips along on his mutilated feet. He does not have to walk far to reach his place of work, which is on the other side of eight railroad tracks. He works in the only place where his presence would not be offensive — among other untouchables like himself. It is Mother Teresa's center for lepers, called

Gandhiji's Prem Nivas, which means "The Ghandi Abode of Love."

John Raju passes through the wards where the most afflicted lepers are lying on their cots and he heads for the workroom of the weavers. He sits down at the loom and with the stumps of his fingers he works at weaving the coarse white cotton cloth that is used for making the saris that are worn by the Missionaries of Charity. For his work John Raju receives 150 rupees a month, a sense of self-respect, and the satisfaction of knowing that he is able to support his family in spite of his disfiguring disease.

John contracted leprosy when he was eight years old; he is now 49. He did not know that he was sick until a Missionary of Charity discovered a nodule on his neck. He was 22 years old when the leprosy was diagnosed and treated in one of Mother Teresa's mobile clinics. It was too late for a complete cure, but the disease was arrested. Nevertheless, John had to leave his work as a receptionist in one of the government offices and be confined to the leper colony at Titagarh. There he married Agnes, who was also a leper, and they had two sons, Taylor and Francis.

The two boys are safe. The Missionaries of Charity had taken them away from their parents immediately, a painful but necessary separation to protect them from contagion. Taylor is now 16 years old and attends a trade school, preparing to be a mechanical engineer. Francis has been sent to Udayan, a center for children of lepers, about 18 miles from Calcutta. He is under observation because of some spots on his back. Meanwhile, he is studying to be a tailor.

Agnes and John Raju live alone and they are happy that their sons have a different kind of life. Their home is a basement room with no windows, no fireplace, and no beds. On the smoke-stained walls there are two movie posters and a photograph of their wedding, taken when Agnes' nose had not yet become leonine and John's fingers were still intact.

As soon as John leaves for work in the morning, Agnes takes her nanny-goat to browse among the bushes along the railroad tracks. She looks both ways to be sure that there is no train coming and there is no policeman to wave his stick at her and motion for her to return immediately to the leper colony.

Not even Mother Teresa knows how many lepers of Calcutta she and her Missionaries of Charity have cared for throughout the years. In the first few years she kept a count, interested as she is in numbers, and the count reached 42,000. But then the numbers exploded and it was impossible to keep up with them. Mother Teresa has replaced numbers with a brief statement: "In Calcutta we have gathered together many thousands of lepers. I assure you that they are wonderful, in spite of their disfigurement." The lepers are the poorest of the poorest of the poor, and for that reason they are especially loved by Mother Teresa. There are centers in Calcutta for the treatment of leprosy, but those who go there are in an advanced stage, are sent by the Board of Health, or are simply alert enough to recognize the first symptoms and sufficiently responsible to seek an early cure. Leprosy is considered a stigma that must be kept hidden, because it provokes social and family rejection, the loss of employment, and eventually banishment to a leper colony. Today the lepers are no longer required to wear a bell attached to their leg so that people can turn away at their approach, but the bell survives nevertheless in the horror that the word "leprosy" arouses.

* * * * *

Mother Teresa, practical as always, decided to care for the lepers in the place where they live, and to do so efficiently and with discretion. At first she thought to do this by means of a mobile dispensary. She requested the first one in 1955 from Father Alfred Schneider, Director of the Catholic Relief Services, an American organization for aid to the Third World. He put $25,000 at her disposal, and an Indian mechanical engineer, Fall

Manekshaw, transformed a van into a mobile clinic. Mother Teresa then sent the mobile unit into the poverty-stricken quarters of the city in search of mothers with leprosy and their children.

The following year an incident convinced Mother Teresa that she should care not only for the mothers and children, but for all lepers. The incident is described by Eileen Egan in her book, *Such a Vision of the Street*:

> One day in 1957, five lepers appeared at the Motherhouse of the Missionaries of Charity. Their dread secret had been discovered and they had been thrown out of their jobs. No one can take them in, not even their own families. Cast off by everyone, they knocked on Mother Teresa's door. This was a sign for her that she must do more for the lepers. The mobile clinic became the vehicle, literally and figuratively, for a new service to those who, more than all the others, deserved the description "the poorest of the poor."
>
> "We used to have a leper hospital right in Calcutta, Gobra Hospital," said Mother Teresa, "but they have closed it down. That's why we have to go to them. There were places for them to report, but many did not. The poor spread the disease and their children are finished. Then there are the ones who are not poor. When their secret is found out, then life is impossible. Men have told me that they have had to leave home and just disappear. Their daughters would never get husbands if they stayed home. Their sons would not get jobs" (pp. 76-77).

In spite of popular prejudice, Mother Teresa launched an all-out campaign, aided by friends and collaborators that included government officials, teachers, wives of businessmen, diplomats, and other persons of good will. They were all won over by the charm of the little Albanian Sister who had made India her second motherland. The symbol of the campaign was a bell, the traditional trademark of lepers, and the slogan was a re-wording of the ancient taboo: "Touch a leper with your compassion." The friends of Mother Teresa stood on the street corners, ringing a bell, distributing leaflets on which the slogan was printed, and soliciting contributions.

A clipping from *The Calcutta Statesman* of September 27, 1957, illustrates the results of the campaign. Under a photo of Archbishop Perier and Mother Teresa, the following explanation is given:

> Mother Teresa's Mobile Leprosy Clinic was opened by the Archbishop of Calcutta, His Grace, the Most Rev. Dr. Ferdinand Perier, at Shishu Bhavan on Lower Circle Road, on Wednesday. A mobile van with medicines and equipment will visit four centres weekly in the four poorest areas in Calcutta — Howrah, Tiljala, Dhappa and Moti Jihl — from where Mother Teresa and her Sisters of Charity have received requests for leprosy treatment. The services of a doctor who has received training for this work in the School for Tropical Medicine has been retained. Three nuns who have received training in nursing patients suffering from leprosy will assist him. A small laboratory has been set up at Shishu Bhavan. There are about 30,000 leprosy patients in Calcutta.

Today Mother Teresa's mobile units travel all over Calcutta. As soon as they park in a place, a line of sick people immediately forms. A volunteer doctor receives the patients in the little laboratory and a Missionary of Charity keeps the records and dispenses the prescribed medicines. Painted on the door of each van is a bell within a blue circle, the ancient symbol of the taboo.

* * * * *

Later on, in addition to the mobile units, Mother Teresa constructed some permanent centers for lepers. In 1959 she opened the center at Titagarh, directly in front of the leper colony, and placed it under the direction of the male branch of the Missionaries of Charity. On October 2, 1975, the anniversary of the birth of Gandhi, Mother named the leprosarium at Titagarh in his honor: *Gandhiji's Prem Nivas*, which means "The Gandhi Abode of Love."

The suffix "ji" is a sign of love and respect. It is customary for the people of India to express their sentiments and to add terms of affection to a person's name. For example, *dapu* for father, *mata* for mother, *dada* for brother, and *didi* for sister. Several times when people stopped to greet Mother Teresa, I heard them say *Mataji, Mataji*, which is a very affectionate term for Mother. In dedicating the leprosarium at Titagarh to Gandhi, Mother Teresa was honoring the apostle of non-violence. Gandhi had called the lepers "children of God." He had also preached against egoism: "There is enough in the world for the needs of all, but there is not enough for the greediness of each one." He urged Christians to live Christ's Sermon on the Mount instead of just preaching it. He understood the value of the suffering of the innocent; he called it *Satyagraha*, the power of truth. He believed in *Madhurya Pradhana Bhakti*, love based on the discovery of the infinite sweetness of God. There is therefore a spiritual bond between Mother Teresa and Mahatma Gandhi that transcends their diversity of religion and temporal span. In India they can both rightly be called *mahatma*, which means "great soul." Perhaps the least publicized honor that India has bestowed on Mother Teresa, but one that was greatly appreciated by her, was the invitation to lay the cornerstone of the *Gandhi Bhavan*, an institute for the study of Gandhi's teaching. The ceremony took place at Allahabad in 1976, and Mother Teresa said on that occasion: "May God bless your beautiful work of diffusing the teaching of Gandhi concerning love and peace." One newspaper stated: "Gandhi is a _karma yogi_ who transforms contemplation into action. Mother Teresa is a _karma yogin_."

* * * * *

In addition to her mobile clinics and the leprosarium _Gandhiji's Prem Nivas_, Mother Teresa has manifested her ability as an evangelizer of the Gospel by establishing a village for lepers. It is about 200 miles from Calcutta and is called _Shanti Nagar_ or "Village of Peace." The four-hour train ride to the village takes one through rice fields that are withered from the drought, and in the last part of the journey one passes through a tunnel of tropical forest. But _Shanti Nagar_ is an oasis of avenues and flower-beds, thanks to Sister Francis Xavier's passion for gardening. A native of Yugoslavia and a doctor of medicine, she has been director of the _Shanti Nagar_ since its beginning. The "Village of Peace" occupies 34 acres of land provided by the Bengali government and paid for by contributions from India and foreign countries. It is Mother Teresa's answer to the ill-famed leper colonies under government supervision, where lepers are confined and then left to themselves without any care. The patients are left to suffer the curse of their disease, which will more than likely be contracted by their children. The government colonies are veritable ghettoes from which no one ever leaves and into which no healthy person would dare enter. Strictly speaking, the "Village of Peace" is not a leper colony; it is a self-sufficient village. The lepers mix freely with the healthy, many of whom are volunteer workers. The more serious cases are cared for in the hospital; the others live with their families in huts that are small but neat and clean. Babies that are born in _Shanti Nagar_ have a safe nest and later on they go to school. They grow up healthy as a rule because they are constantly checked by the doctors and the nursing Sisters. Everybody works — in the stores or the workshops, in tending to the pigs and chickens, or in the fields, cultivating lentils and other vegetables.

* * * * *

India is an attraction for those who want to live the Lord's Sermon on the Mount instead of merely preaching it, as Gandhi had suggested. And Mother Teresa's charm also attracts many to follow her example. I have known two such cases: a successful French writer and an English textile manufacturer. The French writer is Dominique Lapierre and he is a dynamo of ideas and energy. The English manufacturer is James Stevens, who gave up his business to become an Anglican priest. Lapierre founded a movement to aid the children of lepers, and with the contributions he financed a village where the children are housed and cared for and taught a trade or craft. Stevens is the director of the village, which is called *Udayan*, meaning "resurrection." It is located in the tropical forest, about 18 miles from Calcutta, and has a population of 200 children, ranging in age from six to sixteen.

I visited Udayan with Dominique Lapierre and his wife. Spotlessly clean infants and children, dressed in white blouses and blue trousers, welcomed us in Indian fashion: leis of *rajani gandha*, tuberous white flowers with a fragrance that is overpowering; the *tilak*, the good luck streak of red dust on the forehead; the *namaskar*, the traditional greeting with folded hands held in front of the face.

The children of lepers remain at Udayan for about ten years. There are Hindus, Muslims and Christians, and they all pray together, reciting verses from the *Bhagavad Gita*, the Koran and the Bible. After completing the elementary grades, they go on to high school outside the village, or they learn a craft within the village. There are departments of painting and sculpture, music, sewing. In Western Bengal the professions of sculpting, painting and tailoring are held in high regard.

The older children take turns working in the kitchen, cultivating the fields, and raising chickens. In the shade of a fig tree some children are digging a fish pond for raising *rui* and *katla*, spiny sweet-water fish that are very tasty. The heart of Udayan is the dispensary, a red house that stands in a circle of coconut palm trees. It is under the direction of Dr. Bhruba Prasad Sen, a specialist in tropical diseases. He told me: "For thousands of years people believed that leprosy was a curse from God. No, it is not a curse; it is an infectious disease of chronic development, caused by a bacillus called *micro bacterium leprae*, also known as the Hansen bacillus, after the Norwegian doctor who discovered it in 1873. It is not known how the bacillus is transmitted, but it certainly flourishes where there is human poverty, malnutrition, misery, filth, or prolonged contact with lepers who are contagious. For that reason it is absolutely essential to take away the babies of leprous parents. Mother Teresa understood that immediately, however painful and cruel it may seem to separate infants from their parents.

"The most contagious form of leprosy is the type called *lepromatosa*; it infects one fourth of all lepers. There are fifteen million lepers in the world, of which four million are in India alone. We treat the disease with a combination of three antibiotics. Twenty years ago we used a sulfone drug, but the bacillus developed a resistance to it. However, if caught in time, leprosy can be cured within two years."

* * * * *

Dr. Sen's assistant is a young man named Swapan Kumar Naiya, one of the first boys to be admitted to Udayan. After his cure he studied at the anti-leprosy center in Calcutta and became a paramedic. He returned to work full-time at Udayan. His story is the same as many others.

"I was born in Yajanagar of a peasant family of two brothers and five sisters. Leprosy came into our family through my grandmother, and with leprosy came fear. At one time lepers were obliged by law to go around with a bell. That is no longer the case, but the ostracizing continues; you cannot go to school, you cannot find work, you can get married, but only to another leper, and you must live in a leper colony.

"Out of all my brothers and sisters, I am the only one infected with leprosy. I was 12 years old when a white spot appeared on my face. Mother Teresa's missionaries, who go around in a white van, noticed it and immediately separated me from my family and placed me here. As a result, they saved my life. I am now married and my wife is named Chaabi Nama. I met her in the organization called BAM, which means 'Brothers of All Men.' We have a baby girl named Annash who is three years old."

There is a line of silent boys waiting at the entrance to the dispensary, as is the case every morning. Swapan calls the first boy in and checks his health card. There is a nodule on his thigh and the flesh beneath it is insensitive. Meanwhile, Swapan continues speaking to me. "My grandmother was treated with hot water and disinfectant, but it did no good. Her fingers and toes fell off and she developed the leonine nose. She called the disease the curse of Siva. We are Hindus and the Siva is our goddess of destruction. She has five faces, a serpent coiled around her neck, and she wears a necklace of skulls. Today we know that leprosy is not a curse; the true curse of leprosy is fear. I shall teach my daughter Annash not to be afraid."

During the years that she established houses outside of India, Mother Teresa discovered that there is also a "leprosy of the Western World." It is the leprosy of loneliness. She once said: "There are medicines and cures for every disease, but for one who is lonely and unwanted, there is no cure. This is the leprosy of the West." She wants the Missionaries of Charity in the metropolitan centers of the affluent world — New York, San Francisco, London, Rome, Berlin — to concentrate principally on visiting and helping women who are lonely, old people who are lonely, young people who are lonely, the unwanted, the marginalized, the rejected. For this kind of leprosy no one else has time or concern.

MISSIONARIES TO PRISONS

I am climbing up a spiral staircase on the outside of an old building five stories high, plodding behind the white sari of Sister Dionysia, who is already at the top while I am only halfway up. I am afraid of vertigo, of the rusty stairs that are held together by metal bands, and of the crows that stare at me from the branches of a mango tree that they cohabit with the sparrows. From Ripon Street rises the stench of the sewage drain, the odor of boiling olive oil used by the vendor of the *dalpuries*, the fragrance of the flowers in a nearby temple. India assails your nose most of all.

When I painfully reach the roof of the building, Sister Dionysia has already disappeared into a garret that is the airy dwelling for a family of five children and a pensioned couple. They all live together, like the crows and the sparrows. Nehru used to say: "Calcutta is a nightmare." It is both a nightmare and a miracle. Since most Indians are slight of build and have an almost infinite capacity for tolerance, they can live in a space no larger than a closet or adjust to living in dens and small openings as if they were made of cartilage instead of bones. Indeed, they seem to contradict the law of the impenetrability of bodies. In Calcutta space is at a premium. I noticed this when I accompanied Sister Dionysia to various "houses" that are not big enough to merit the name.

I had asked Mother Teresa if I could accompany a Missionary of Charity on her rounds and I was assigned to Sister Dionysia. She is something of a paramedic, social worker, spiritual counselor and contemplative all rolled in one, as are the rest of Mother Teresa's Sisters. It is the day on which Sister Dionysia visits families and she carried a shopping bag full of medicines, a pad to jot down the more urgent cases, and a rosary for praying as she makes her rounds. She is a robust and joyful person, and she had given me a copy of her weekly schedule so that I could choose the day that I wanted to accompany her. Mondays and Tuesdays she was assigned to the consulting room at Sealdah; Wednesdays, the tuberculosis dispensary; Thursdays and Fridays, family counseling; Saturdays, house-cleaning in the home for the aged; Sundays, visitation of families being helped. I chose Sunday.

* * * * *

> *Every day is a kind of miracle.*
> *Not a day passes that there is not some gentle attention*
> *from God, a sign of his solicitude.*
> *The greatest miracle is that God is served by little beings*
> *such as we. He uses us to do his work.*
> *Let God use you without consulting you.*

Mother Teresa

* * * * *

The home of the two sisters, Margaret and Joyce Gonsalves, is in the basement of a building that dates from the 1800's. It is nothing more than a closet that was once used by the servants as a storeroom for brooms and buckets. The eldest of Margaret's four children, Clinton, has tuberculosis. Sister Dionysia places on the table the bottles of the monthly dosage of medicine. Then she notes on her pad: "Send milk and nourishing crackers." This is the first of the "stations of the cross" that we visit today.

Sister Dionysia had promised to tell me the story of her life during the spare moments of our rounds. She began in the Gonsalves home. "I was born in Paingotoor in Kerala, in southern India, in 1952. My father was a doctor and there were eight brothers and sisters in the family. When I was 12 years old, they spoke about Mother Teresa in school. Pope Paul VI had given her the Cadillac that he had used at the Eucharistic Congress in Bombay in December of 1964. It had been given to him by the University of Notre Dame in South Bend, Indiana.

"Mother Teresa did not know what to do with the automobile; she called it a 'white elephant.' If she could have transformed it into an ambulance or a van for transporting goods, she would have kept it. But that was impossible. Then she thought of conducting a raffle. She collected 460,000 rupees with the sale of tickets, an enormous amount of money. The Cadillac was won by a Mr. Parsi, who immediately sold it and gave Mother Teresa half of the sale price.

"Our teacher told us this story, reading from an article in the newspaper. I was greatly impressed. I would have liked to know that Sister, but living so far away from Calcutta, I wondered how I could do so. Finally, at the age of 16, I decided to write to her, with the help of my father. I asked her to accept me as a Missionary of Charity.

"Mother answered immediately. My hands were trembling as I opened the letter, but I wept when I read the response: 'You are too young. Study. Pray. Then we shall see.' That's what she wrote.

"When I was 18, with my father's permission I boarded the train, and after two nights and a day of travel, I arrived at Calcutta. Mother Teresa welcomed me with an embrace and said: 'Ah, now it is a serious matter and not a passing infatuation.' When I put on the habit of a postulant, all white but without the blue border, I experienced a joy that I had never felt before."

* * * * *

What strikes people and causes some of them to embrace the religious life is the witness of our lives, the spirit with which we respond to the divine call, the totality of our dedication, the generosity and joy that we manifest in serving God, the mutual love, the apostolic zeal with which we bear witness to the love of Christ for the poorest of the poor.

When you smile, my dear novices, I can hear the music of your smile. Learn how to be holy, my daughters, because true holiness consists in doing God's will with a smile.

I remember that some time ago more than 40 professors from various universities came to visit us.... One of them asked in the name of the others: "Mother, tell us something that will help us to transform our lives."

I replied: "Smile at one another."

Then one of them asked me: "Are you married?"

"Yes," I answered, "and sometimes I find it difficult to smile at Jesus, because he is very demanding."

Mother Teresa

* * * * *

"I pronounced my vows in 1978 and I began to work at Shishu Bhavan, taking care of adoptions. In three years time we gave out 600 babies for adoption, 200 of which went to Italy. No, we do not consider one type of work better than another. All works are better. In May of 1981, Mother sent me to open a new house at Kearchand, which is three hours travel from Calcutta. In 1983 we inaugurated Shanta Bhavan, the home for infants at Darjeeling.

We had a very cold winter there and many infants died of pneumonia. A man who is a Buddhist gave us a three-story building with about six acres of ground. It had been abandoned for a long time and was almost overrun by the forest. There were only four of us, I as the superior and three other Sisters. How did we manage? We prayed; and in response to our prayers, Father Beckers, a professor at the Jesuit University in Calcutta, telephoned to tell me that he would come to give us a hand, together with about 20 students from the university. As soon as he arrived, he took off his shirt and chopped down five trees. Following the example of the students from Calcutta, the boys from the local school vied with them in helping us clear the land, paint the house and put it in order.

"In 1987 Mother appointed me director of the novices, and I became regional superior. Yes, one quickly makes a 'career' in our Congregation, although we do not use the word 'career.' We are not attached to anything, and we always start again from nothing." Sister Dionysia laughs, and her infectious joy causes the others to laugh as well: Mary O'Cruze, her three children and her niece Priscilla, who is a very beautiful girl. But then, all the girls in India are beautiful, until pregnancy and drudgery transform them into old women at the age of 30.

We are now at Number 2 on Sandal Street, where the eight members of the O'Cruze family live in two rooms. Their quarters are at street level, and when the monsoon rains come, a torrent of water invades the house and everything floats around the room. A monsoon is about to arrive, and the O'Cruze family has set up a brick barrier on the threshold. Sister Dionysia tells them that will cause even more problems because the water will pass over the barrier and then it cannot flow back into the street. She tells them to place the bricks under the legs of the table and the cots to keep them above the water level.

* * * * *

Do not look for spectacular works. What is important is the gift of yourselves. What matters is the degree of love that you put into your every deed.

Our Sisters do little things: they take care of infants; they visit those who live in loneliness; the sick, and those who lack everything.

When someone tells me that what the Sisters do is of little importance, that they are limited to doing what is less than ordinary, I answer that even if they help only one person, that would be a sufficient motive for their work.

Jesus would have died for one single person.

Be faithful in little things, because it is there that your strength lies.

Nothing is little that is done for God.

Mother Teresa

* * * * *

"In 1989 I returned to Calcutta to take charge of the Sisters who are preparing for their final vows. Then, in 1990, Mother entrusted a new mission to me: to begin an apostolate to the women in the prison at Tengra.

"The prison is near the airport. In the women's section there are not only criminals, but women found by the police in the street in a confused state, and young girls who have come to Calcutta from the countryside. Frequently they get lost in the crowds and cannot find their way home. The authorities don't know where to send them, so they place them 'temporarily' in the prison and then forget about them.

"When a newspaper denounced this practice, Mother decided that we should do something for those unhappy individuals. She entrusted the task to me. I did not know how to begin, but Mother said to me: 'Pray to the Blessed Virgin Mary; you will see that she will help you'."

* * * * *

The Madonna is the most beautiful of all women, the greatest, the most humble, the most pure, the most holy.

When she felt herself inundated with grace, full of Jesus, 'she went in haste.' I think that is the reason why God chose a woman to manifest his love and compassion for the world.

We also, like Mary, should go in search of our children, as she did when Jesus was lost.

Mother Teresa

* * * * *

"I prayed to the Madonna. A Hindu woman came for me and accompanied me by car to Tengra. We spoke with the director of the prison and obtained permission to enter the women's section. There were about 300 women consigned to one room, forced to sleep on the ground. They were dishevelled and undernourished and dressed in filthy rags, the sick mixed with the healthy and the innocent with criminals. We protested to the director and he told us that he was not responsible for such conditions; he was simply obeying the order of the court to keep them in custody. The prison is what it is, a prison."

That's the way the work of Sister Dionysia began at the prison in Tengra. She obtained a permanent permission from the director and spent hours with the prisoners, gaining their confidence, listening to their history and their confused recollections. She became a kind of detective, making inquiries at the court and the police stations, challenging the frustrating Indian bureaucracy, and placing announcements and photos of missing persons in the newspapers.

And now, during a break in our visitation of families, we are seated in a pew in St. Mary's Church beneath a ventilating fan that circulates the hot air. Sister Dionysia sums up for me the results of her investigation and efforts. "I am working on approximately 70 cases. Up until now I have obtained the release of 23 girls who came to Calcutta from the country and were lost. I have located the families of seven women who are mentally disturbed. They had wandered away from home and were unable to find their way back. The road they have travelled is unbelievable, wandering around for months before reaching Calcutta. One had family at Burdwan, another at Assam, one in a village on the frontier of Bangladesh, still another in the suburbs of Calcutta, and one at Hyderabad."

Sister Dionysia would like to have told me the story of each case, but we had been walking for hours and she had to return home. Mother Teresa insists that the Sisters should always eat together unless prevented by an emergency. With a motherly concern she is anxious about them because they are on their feet all day, starting at 4:30 in the morning. By noon they have already spent seven hours at work and in prayer; moreover, the second half of the day still awaits them. She wants them to sit at table and share with one another the experiences of the morning. Then they have a half hour of repose before they set out again at two o'clock in the afternoon.

* * * * *

> *To be able to do what they do, to live as they do, our Sisters give themselves to the love of Christ with a heart protected by chastity, with the freedom of poverty, with whole-hearted obedience, in total service to the poorest of the poor and to Christ under the suffering aspect of the poor.*
>
> *To be able to live this life of ours, we must have a great love for the Eucharist.*
>
> *We begin the journey of each day with Jesus, and in the evening we have an hour of adoration of him exposed in the Eucharist. Our daily twelve hours of service to the poor are not seen as an interruption of this. The hour of adoration is the greatest gift.*

Mother Teresa

* * * * *

As we walk hurriedly along Ripon Street, groups of children surround us. There is a fluttering of little hands and expectant glances as they enact the pantomime of begging. They place three fingers on their forehead in greeting and then three fingers on their mouth, signifying "I am hungry," then again three fingers on their forehead as a sign of gratitude in advance. Sister Dionysia extends her arms as if to say that she has nothing to give them except a smile. For my part, by this time I have learned the lesson of indifference, which serves as a protection against the abyss of misery in India. As we continue walking, Sister Dionysia tells me two stories about the women in the prison at Tengra.

"Yadamma came from Hyderabad. She was a middle-aged woman, quiet and happy with her family, which consisted of a husband and two children. They were poor farmers, but not any poorer than most of the farmers in India. When her husband left her without giving a reason, Yadamma began to suffer emotional disturbances.

"One day, in a confused state, she left the house and boarded a train. Perhaps she wanted to go in search of her husband. When she got off the train at Calcutta, she was completely disoriented and didn't know where she was. She slept on the sidewalk at night and during the day she wandered through the streets, looking for food in the garbage. The police finally found her in a state of extreme agitation and they brought her to the prison at Tengra. Nobody asked her what her name was or where she came from. Nobody made any inquiries to locate her family. For two years she lived in that prison like an animal.

"I went to the director and told him that we Sisters would take care of her, so he gave permission for her release. She was dishevelled and half naked, and she had a lost look in her eyes. We washed and fed her, and eventually she regained something of a human appearance and began to talk.

"After many inquiries, we were able to locate her family. They had desperately searched for her everywhere and they

79

never gave up the search. They could not have imagined that she would end up in a prison in Calcutta, which is very far from their home. Three members of the family came to fetch her: her mother, her brother and one of her sons. I shall never forget the tears of Yadamma when she saw her loved ones or the last peaceful look that she gave me from the window of the train."

* * * * *

The poor have no need of our pity. The poor need our help and assistance. What they give us is more than we give them. Christ said: "I was hungry and you gave me to eat." He hungered not only for bread but for love that makes one understand that one is loved, is known, is somebody for someone. He was naked not only in reference to clothing but also in reference to human dignity, because of the injustice that is done to the poor, who are disdained simply because they are poor. Christ knew the abandonment of those in prison, those who are rejected, those who are not wanted, those who walk through this world devoid of all help.

Mother Teresa

* * * * *

"Fazila was the daughter of a farmer who came regularly to Calcutta to sell rice. One day her father decided to take her along to see the big city. She was then 11 years old. In the train station at Sealdah, she was enchanted by the large crowds of people. She got separated from her father and was swallowed up in the crowd. The police found her three days later, hungry and desperate. Not knowing where to put her, they brought her to the prison at Tengra. Nobody was concerned about her, and when I first met her, she had been in prison for ten years. That's unbelievable, isn't it? Neither did I believe it when she told me, but it was true. Fazila is a beautiful girl, tall, with large eyes. Having grown up in that inferno, she had forgotten everything. She no longer knew how to write, her speech was almost unintelligible, she was even afraid of the light and the fresh air. We kept her with us for six months, re-educating her for human contacts. Finally, one day she remembered a name: Boshirghat. It was the name of the locality that she had left with her father ten years before.

"Fazila and I were on the train the next day. We left at nine in the morning, and four hours later we descended at Boshirghat. There, Fazila remembered that once she had been on a boat on the river and then she also remembered the name of her village: Pakaidanga. So we boarded a boat that goes to the villages in the interior, and when we disembarked, we were in the midst of the tropical forest. It began to get dark and to rain heavily. We had not eaten since early morning. We walked and walked, carrying our sandals so we would not lose them in the mud, and we finally arrived at a village. We asked the first persons we met where Pakaidanga was, and we also told them that we were looking for the parents of a girl who had been lost ten years ago.

"Word got around and people came out of their huts. They walked along with us, forming a procession that marched from village to village. As we approached Pakaidanga, some people ran ahead to notify the parents. We advanced, surrounded by a crowd in which there were many girls. Fazila's father and mother stopped in front of the first girls, shouting, now at one, then at another: 'It is this one.... It is this one,' until I was able to make my way forward and cry out: 'No, this is Fazila.'"

THE SCANDAL OF INDIA

An obsession with the poor. A passion for the poor. The poor exist all over, but only in India do they take your breath away. Would Mother Teresa have become what she is — the universal symbol of mercy — if instead of disembarking at Calcutta, she had remained at Rathfarnham in Ireland or if her superior had sent her as a missionary to some other country? It's an idle question. Mother Teresa became a Sister precisely to go to India as a missionary. Her calling was to India, and it came to her early in life, a very urgent and demanding calling that only India could satisfy.

Mother Teresa returned to her native town in 1978, fifty years after she had left it. At the airport in Skopje a crowd awaited her; they had come by bus at the break of dawn. In the front line were the journalists, the TV crew and the cameramen from Vradan Films in the hope of making a documentary. No sooner had Mother Teresa descended from the plane than they all ran towards the tarmac. The people wanted to touch her, to embrace her, to speak with her, disregarding the efforts of the police to restrain them. It took an hour for Mother Teresa to extricate herself from the crowd. She took the time to say to the journalists: "I was 17 years old when I left Skopje. I studied here in the high school but then suddenly I left our country to give help to others. Now I return, after 50 years. Everything is changed, but it is better that way." As was her custom, she spoke succinctly and somewhat brusquely.

"Suddenly I left our country." Suddenly, but not blindly. She responded to the call of India and followed that call along the mysterious ways of God's providence. In 1925, Agnes Bojaxhiu, age 15 and a high school student, attended the Sodality meetings with her friends. The Sodality was a Catholic club that provided recreation, a choir, theater and excursions. One Sunday afternoon the members of the Sodality met with some missionaries who had come from Bengal. The young people did not know where Bengal was, so the missionaries pointed it out to them on a map. They also spoke about the challenges and the hardships of their work and described the natural disasters and the incredible poverty in India. Some months later, a letter from Kurseong, Western Bengal, arrived at the Sodality. The missionaries described the latest disaster: "As a result of the monsoon, the rivers are overflowing their banks. The water carries with it snakes and cows as well as scores of corpses and injured persons clinging to tree trunks. We have held out poles and thrown out ropes.... We have saved some people. Now we are taking care of the survivors as best we can, but we are few."

"But we are few."

So Agnes decided to become a missionary to India. She investigated and she discovered a religious institute that was just right for her because it sends missionaries to India. It is the Congregation of Our Lady of Loreto, and its Motherhouse is in Rathfarnham, County Dublin, Ireland. Agnes wrote a letter, asking to be admitted to the community. Later on, Mother Teresa recalled: "At the beginning, Mama was opposed to my vocation as a missionary, although she was a holy woman. She did not want to lose me. Everybody in the family prayed together. One day Mama said to me: 'I will give you permission; then go.' And what did she do? She locked herself in her room and for a whole day she refused to see anybody. That evening she said to me: 'Put your hand in the hand of Jesus and look ahead. Never look back. Always ahead.' And that it what I have done."

When she left her home for Ireland, Agnes had just completed her eighteenth year; it was September 25, 1928. She stayed at Rathfarnham for two months, impatient to set out for India, but she used the time to verify her vocation and to study English. On December 1, 1928, she sailed for India on the ship *Marcha*, and on January 6, 1929, she sent her first article to the Yugoslav magazine, *The Catholic Missions*, describing the impact that "the land of my dreams" made on her.

> At Madras I witnessed the sad spectacle of that poor people.... Many families live on the street along the wall of the city and in the crowded squares. They live in the open, day and night, and they sleep on mats made out of the large leaves of palm trees or even on the bare ground. They are almost naked, with a tattered cloth around their waist. One family was mourning a dead parent. The body was wrapped in red cloth and covered with yellow flowers, and there were colored stripes painted on the face. If our people could only see all that, they would be moved to sorrow for their own ingratitude and would thank God for having blessed them with such an abundance.

* * * * *

An obsession with the poor. A passion for the poor. That young girl of eighteen was already committed. Then why did she wait so long before going out to live among the poor? How could she live for almost twenty years in the comfort of Entally with that concern for the poor which long ago had begun to gnaw at her soul? What caused her suddenly to make the shocking decision to put aside the black habit of Loreto and don the white sari? Why did she spend a decade of her twenty years and then almost a decade of her thirty years — the most significant years of life — teaching in the classroom like the rest of her companions? Why did her vocation need so much time to develop and come to fruition? Is this the mystery of Mother Teresa?

These questions were turning over in my mind as I made my way to the residence of the Archbishop of Calcutta on Park Street. And what I found inside did not help me find any answers.

On both sides of Park Street, the most elegant street in the city, entire families have made the sidewalk their home. Their kitchen is an open fire, their bedroom is a tattered piece of cloth that serves as a blanket at night and by day provides some protection against the monsoon rains or the scorching heat of the sun. Their means of sustenance are ingenuous: the women walk around the streets, carrying their small babies on their hips and, with the help of the bigger children, they collect the *ghute*, the cow dung that is used as fuel for the fire. They place the *ghute* in the sun to dry and then sell it for 10 rupees per basket. A journalist once told me: "The *ghute* is the coat of arms of Calcutta."

The men of the family go to the market to look for discards and then recycle them for their little street stands, putting them in little piles on the ground, arranged according to their "quality." They sell their products to other poor people at prices marked in *daisa*, which is one-hundredth of a rupee. Thus, a bunch of grapes will cost 30 *daisa* if the grapes are only slightly bruised; 20 *daisa* if half of the grapes are spoiled. There are also small piles of coal that have been extracted from the fires of the *ghat*, the cremation of the dead. The coal can be recycled for cooking and the prices vary, depending on whether the coal is only slightly burned, half burned or almost entirely reduced to ashes. Then there are the little bunches of flowers that are offered in the temple of the gods during the *pujah*, a sacred ceremony which even the most wretchedly poor Hindu would not dare to omit. The white tuberose and the red hibiscus that are thrown out at the end of the market day are put up again for sale by the sidewalk vendors. Once again, the prices vary, depending on whether the flowers are somewhat faded, quite faded or withered.

The street-dwellers themselves are also of various types. Some are emaciated but still able to provide for their daily sustenance; others are sick or deformed and have to live by begging alms; still others are in the last stages and waiting for death. Each morning the police vans make the rounds of the city to collect those who have died during the night. Usually I try to avoid these scenes of human misery by keeping a safe distance or by going around the city by taxi. Today, however, I am looking for answers to my questions, so I look at the scenes of suffering as long as I can without getting nauseated. On this day, at least, I do not wrap myself in the protective covering of indifference. I must know how India brought Mother Teresa to the point of making her revolutionary decision.

* * * * *

The Archbishop's residence is too strong a contrast. I observe closely the graceful Bengali architecture and ornamentation, the trees and bushes with their new leaves of brilliant green, the bubbling fountain at which the crows and sparrows are drinking, the grotto of Our Lady of Lourdes, the lushness of tropical vegetation speckled with dahlias and Canterbury bells as big as sunflowers, the garden of fresh, plump tomatoes. I ask myself, without having any right to do so, whether it is possible to live in paradise just a few steps away from hell. Henry D'Souza, Archbishop of Calcutta, is a heavy-set man with white hair contrasting sharply with his dark-complexioned face. There are two dark blotches beneath his cheek-bone, something typically Indian. He is about 50 years old and he has the dignity of a Brahmin and the gentleness of a *guru*, which is also typically Indian.

"How can you live here, Archbishop, when the people outside...?"

"Ah, I know well your reaction. It is the reaction of all Westerners who come to India. India upsets people. India exceeds all limits. India forces one either to close one's eyes or to open them wide and stare.

"Look, I was born in India. No, that is not an excuse; I became a priest in order not to close my eyes. I went to the seminary; I was ordained a priest; I became a pastor and then a bishop. I have always been confronted with poverty; it is the tragedy of India. I am also trying to face it from my position. I know I am inadequate, but God commands us through signs.

"Mother Teresa is a sign and a teacher. She is a sign for us on how to respond to poverty, and her example serves to stimulate and multiply initiatives. I call her Mother twice over."

I had come to ask the Archbishop what Mother Teresa has done for India and what India has done for Mother Teresa. But first of all, Archbishop D'Souza wanted to explain why he had said that for him Mother Teresa is mother twice over.

"A short time before my ordination to the priesthood, I had the sad experience of losing my mother. She had always dreamed of seeing me a priest, but she was not here at the precise time that her dream was fulfilled. I said to Mother Teresa: 'Make me this promise: "I will be at your ordination".'

"I did not count on it too much, because I knew how many affairs she has to take care of during her travels around the world. But when I entered the cathedral on ordination day in the procession of concelebrants, I saw Mother Teresa seated next to my father. She smiled at me and said simply: 'Here I am.'

"I had known her when I was a seminarian. She often came to the seminary to ask the seminarians to help her in some emergency or other. We were impressed by her total dedication and her promptness in facing up to problems. Later, I met her at

Bhubaneswar, about 30 miles south of Calcutta, where she had opened a house for lepers at the request of the government. But it was when I became pastor at Kharjpur on the outskirts of Calcutta that I could really see what the presence of Mother Teresa in Calcutta meant for the poor. I put all the problems of the poor in her hands. One day she said to me, as a kind of rebuke: 'You always talk about problems. Can't we find another word to describe difficulties?'

"'What word, Mother?'

"'For example, the word *gift.*'

That's the way she is. She spreads serenity with her innate ability to pacify, showing that even in the face of difficulties there are reasons for gratitude. From then on, whenever I called her, I would begin: 'Mother, I want to give you a little *gift*' or 'This time the *gift* is a big one.'

"In 1984 I had a heart attack. Mother Teresa, who was in New York, sent this telegram to me in the hospital: 'Who gave you permission to get sick?' Later, when she herself was recovering from a heart condition in 1989, I rushed to her side and the first thing I said was: 'Mother, who gave you permission to get sick?' She was in serious condition, but she found the strength to laugh.

* * * * *

An obsession with the poor. Passion for the poor. The poor of India, who are present wherever you go, force you to compare the way you live with the horror of their lives. "Why did Mother Teresa wait 20 years before she went among the poor? Do you have an answer, Archbishop?"

"No, I don't, but I can offer a theory. Mother Teresa was eighteen years old when she arrived in India. At that age there may be enthusiasm in the heart but insufficient clarity of one's aims. She arrived in India as a Sister of Loreto, obliged to follow the rule of Loreto. In the succeeding years I can imagine that she was held back by reasons of convenience, obedience or prudence, but eventually she could no longer bear the sights of India.

"India disorients and scandalizes a person. It is necessary to know India deeply in order to understand her. I am an Indian and a Christian, and sometimes my Christianity comes into conflict with my being an Indian. Christianity is based on divine providence, on the certainty of redemption, and on the promise of a resurrection into the peace of Christ. Hinduism rests on *karma*, and *karma* leads to fatalism and resignation.

"We criticize the Hindus for not being concerned about the necessities of life or the suffering of others, preoccupied as they are with their individual spiritual search. Yes, they are contemplatives, but they sincerely admire those who perform good works. The Hindu appreciates Christian charity, just as the Christian appreciates Hindu detachment. The tremendous influence that Gandhi exercised over the Hindu crowds was due in part to his ability to make a synthesis between detachment and charity, between mysticism and compassion. Mother Teresa has also made that synthesis."

* * * * *

The central doctrine of Hinduism is *karmasamsara*, the transmigration of souls according to the perpetual laws of retribution. As a snake changes its skin, so also the human soul passes from one body to another. The soul is a spiritual substance, intellectual and eternal, and it goes through a succession of births and deaths. The previous existences determine its present existence. In one lifetime, however, the human soul accumulates more debts than it can possibly pay, or more rewards than it can possibly collect. The future lives serve to balance the account.

In the *Bhagavad Gita*, the holy book of Hinduism, the body is compared to a field. With every human act a seed falls into the field, a seed that immediately germinates and will bear fruit. If one's actions are noble, there will be a harvest of flowers and good fruit; if the actions are wicked, the harvest will be thorns and weeds. To improve one's destiny, it is necessary to better oneself at the present moment by deepening one's spirituality. Millions of seeds were planted in the field of the body in one's previous life. In due time that previous planting will be harvested and a new planting and harvest will take its place. Consequently, our place in the universe, the tasks assigned to us, our pleasures and pains, happiness and unhappiness, are all determined by _karma_, the inexorable laws of cause and effect.

> It is by one's own actions
> that we merit happiness and sorrow,
> that we are reborn as master or slave,
> that we contract diseases,
> that we receive beauty or deformity....
> This is the very essence
> of the secret of _karma_.
> The knowledge of this wisdom
> is the ship of salvation
> that enables us to traverse
> the ocean of hell.
>
> _Brahmavaivarta Purana_

* * * * *

Archbishop D'Souza commented: "The _karma_ is the great compass for Indian life. If today you are a Brahmin, it is because you did well in your previous life. If you are an untouchable, you are atoning for your past. Do you have leprosy? God is punishing you for your past sins.

"Yes, India has changed Mother Teresa. The impact of its dehumanizing poverty challenged her to take up the cause of the poorest of the poor. But Mother Teresa has also changed

India by challenging in turn its fatalistic mentality and by defending the irreplaceable value of the human person.

"God loves you — that is the teaching of Mother Teresa. Leprosy is not a punishment but a curable disease. When Mother Teresa bends over a sick person whose body is covered with sores, she does not judge, she does not accuse of any fault; rather, she restores that person's dignity as a human being. The greater the suffering, the greater the person's value in the eyes of God, that God who became man in order to take upon himself all the suffering of the world. In every person who suffers, Mother Teresa sees the face of Christ, who became incarnate and, though he was without sin, he accepted death on the cross to redeem us from all our sins. In the name of Christ, Mother Teresa insists that every human life is precious.

"Moreover, Mother Teresa is a master at fostering compassion and stimulating generosity. I remember a young Hindu couple whom I knew well. In preparing for their marriage, they asked their parents and friends to give them the money that would have been spent on the celebration and gifts. They received it and then gave it to Mother Teresa. She asked them: 'Why are you making such a sacrifice?' They answered: 'In exchange for this sacrifice, God will protect our love'."

* * * * *

Mother Teresa always says: "I hope that whatever you give me will not come from your surplus but is the fruit of a sacrifice made out of your love for God."

She loves to give little examples: the Hindu child who brought her all the sugar he had saved during the past week instead of putting it in his bowl of milk; the woman who shared with her neighbors the bag of rice she received from the Missionaries of Charity, saying: "They are also hungry." Then there was the beggar who stopped Mother on the street and gave her the alms he had collected that day. "I took the money from his hands and I can tell you that his face was radiant with joy. I can also tell you this: in my heart I felt that I had received from him something greater than the Nobel Peace Prize."

Mother Teresa's philosophy is both simple and profound: the gift should be more profitable to the giver than to the one who receives it. "I do not ask for charity; I have never asked for it, even at the beginning. I go to people — it makes no difference whether they are Hindus, Muslims or Christians — and I say: 'I am giving you an opportunity to do something beautiful for God'."

She doesn't mention the joy of giving, the satisfaction of being a benefactor, the recognition for philanthropy. She seems to have adopted from Hinduism the concept of *niskama seva*, which means a service without recompense. But perhaps she would state it this way: a service that does not demand a recompense and is done at the cost of a sacrifice. "Give until it hurts," she says. "True love should hurt. The cross hurt Jesus."

PIONEER SCOUTS

Mother Teresa was 50 years old when she left India for the first time. The year was 1960. At that time there were 119 Sisters in her Congregation and all but three were Indian.

On August 9 she wrote to her American friend, Eileen Egan: "I have been invited to Las Vegas for the Convention of American Catholic Women. I asked His Grace and he told me that I should go. Therefore, if all goes well and it is really the will of God, I will come for the Convention.... I am glad that I will have the chance to thank personally the greathearted Americans for their love of God's poor."

"His Grace" was Archbishop Ferdinand Perier, the venerable protector of the Missionaries of Charity, who at that time was 85 years old.

It is difficult to imagine a more paradoxical place for the first overseas journey of the Sister of the slums of Calcutta. Las Vegas is the gambling capital of the world. In its casinos, which are open 24 hours a day, a deluge of dollars crosses the roulette and blackjack tables, while the slot machines, called "one-armed bandits," swallow up an equally constant flow of money. Las Vegas is in a sense America's clown face. Near the gambling casinos are chapels where weddings are celebrated day and night at any hour, after a quick divorce in Reno.

The National Council of Catholic Women had selected that

unlikely place to hold their Convention because, in order to present a better face, the city of Las Vegas provided a huge auditorium free of charge for conventions of charitable organizations. Nothing in America is more compelling than the word "free," and the National Council of Catholic Women accepted the offer. One can imagine the amazement of the 3,000 delegates when they arrived at that gambling capital, but more surprising was the number of police at the Los Angeles Airport, where Mother Teresa first set foot on American soil, on October 4, 1960. She had travelled alone, and on disembarking, she presented her Indian passport to the customs official, who looked with some perplexity at the strange little woman dressed in the Indian sari.

"Where are you going?" he asked.

"To Las Vegas."

At that, the official burst out laughing. Mother Teresa said later: "I think he must have thought I was crazy."

During her stay in Las Vegas, there were other unusual incidents, as Eileen Egan, who accompanied her, relates in her book, *Such a Vision of the Street*. For example, Cardinal Cushing of Boston, met her on her arrival in Las Vegas, gave her the nickname "Mahatma Gandhi" as soon as he saw her, and continued to call her by that name during the four days of the Convention.

It was the first time that Mother Teresa gave a public speech and she was frightened. Eileen gave her a photo that had been taken in Calcutta by Sister Shanti, one of the Missionaries of Charity. Mother Teresa, who sees signs in every little gesture, said later that the photo made her calm and courageous because the word *shanti* in Hindu means "peace." Mother Teresa told the 3,000 delegates about her lepers and her sick, about those she had rescued and those she had helped to die with human dignity. Then later, seated at the stand in the exhibit hall, featuring a photographic display of Mother Teresa's various works of peace, she answered questions about her work, the city of Calcutta, and the strange sari with the blue border. On her arm she carried the usual coarse cloth shopping bag, and as she talked, the delegates quietly slipped American dollars into it. The shopping bag had to be emptied time and time again. Meanwhile, Las Vegas pulsated with its customary frenzy of activity. On the "Strip," the main artery of the city, the lights of the casinos, restaurants and night clubs are never extinguished. Each evening Mother Teresa was able to see the bright lights of the city, and when Eileen Egan asked her what she thought of it, she answered in one word: *Dewali*. She was referring to the "feast of lights" with which the Hindu tradition recalls the return of the god Rama. On that feast, every Indian city and village is decorated with candles and colored lights. Mother Teresa brought home a souvenir from Las Vegas. It was a souvenir that only she would have thought of. When she was taken to see the desert, which begins at the edge of the city, she sat in silence at sunset near a cactus. Picking a handful of thorns from the plant she wove them into a crown. That crown is now on the head of Christ crucified, in the chapel of the Motherhouse in Calcutta.

* * * * *

As a conclusion to that first trip outside India, Mother Teresa made a stop at Rome. Before she left for the United States, she had written to the Sisters:

> I go, but my heart and my mind and the whole of me is with you.... I am not afraid to leave you, for I know the great gift God has given me — in giving you to me. On my way back... I shall go to Rome. Begin a novena to the Sacred Heart... I am going to try to see our Holy Father and beg of him to take our little Society under his special care and grant us pontifical recognition. As you know, we are not worthy of this great gift, but if it is God's holy will, we will get it. You pray and make many sacrifices.

During this time it would make me very happy if the seniors make sacrifices in obedience; juniors in charity; novices in poverty; postulants in chastity.

Be faithful in little things, for in them our strength lies.... Yes, my dear children, be faithful in little practices of love, of little sacrifices — of little fidelities to the rule, which will build in you the life of holiness — make you Christlike.

To the feet of Christ's Vicar on earth I will carry each one of you — just as you are — and I am sure that with his fatherly love [he] will bless each one of you and obtain for you the graces you need to become saints.

So Mother Teresa boarded the plane at Las Vegas and headed for Rome, with intermediate stops at Peoria, Illinois, Chicago, Washington, D.C., New York City, London, as well as Aachen and Munich in Germany. She was accompanied by Eileen Egan, and during her stay in Rome, Mother Teresa met Pope John XXIII, Cardinal Agagianian, and her brother Lazar.

* * * * *

The meeting with Pope John XXIII was not a historical one. The Pope advised her to take her petition to Cardinal Agagianian, Cardinal Prefect of the Congregation for the Propagation of the Faith. However, he did invite her to assist at the papal Mass in the Sistine Chapel. As he exited after the Mass, he stopped to bless her. Few persons in the papal entourage knew who that Sister strangely attired in an Indian sari was. But since the time that St. Francis of Assisi entered the papal audience chamber dressed in tattered clothes, the Vatican is no longer surprised at seeing persons dressed in the garb of poverty.

The meeting with Cardinal Agagianian at the office of the Congregation for the Propagation of the Faith in the Piazza di

Spagna was much more profitable. Seated on a red damask chair, Mother Teresa presented her petition. Before dawn she had knocked at Eileen Egan's door and asked her to type two letters that she had written by hand during the night, describing the work of the Missionaries of Charity.

Cardinal Agagianian and Archbishop Pietro Sigismondi read the two pages carefully. They then asked many questions. The Cardinal was amazed that in a mission country the Missionaries of Charity were able to work and survive without a regular flow of funds from outside India. Mother Teresa explained that her Sisters needed very little to live on and that up to now divine providence had always sustained them.

The two prelates then examined the book of prayers used by the Sisters. It was a little book, mimeographed on cheap paper, and in English. The Archbishop whispered to Cardinal Agagianian: "But it doesn't have an *imprimatur*."

The Cardinal threw up his arms and said with ironic good humor: "But they are poor!"

When Eileen Egan, who understood Italian, translated the Cardinal's retort, Mother Teresa smiled in gratitude. Several years later, Eileen Egan wrote in her book on Mother Teresa:

> Remembering this, I took note of a later edition of the prayer book. On its front page were two names of key importance to the Missionaries of Charity:

> Nihil Obstat
> C. Van Exem, S.J.
> 14-8-1962
> Imprimatur
> †Ferdinandus, S.J.
> Archbishop of Calcutta

* * * * *

The meeting with her brother Lazar, her sister-in-law Maria, and her niece Age in Rome was for Mother Teresa a return to her Albanian roots and the affection of her own family. She then left for Calcutta, where she had left "my heart and my mind and the whole of me." She brought a gift for the Sisters: a packet of crucifixes of black wood with the word "Roma" painted on the back. They were given to her by Monsignor Andrew Landi, the head of the Italian section of Catholic Relief Services.

Mother returned to Calcutta very satisfied and she had many things to tell the Sisters: the reaction of the customs officer in the Los Angeles airport, the attendance at the papal Mass in the Sistine Chapel, the meeting with Cardinal Agagianian. The final interesting incident occurred in the airport in Rome while she was waiting to board the plane that would take her back to Calcutta. This is the way Eileen Egan describes it in her book, *Such a Vision of the Street*:

> When we arrived at the Rome airport, an Indian woman in a striking cream and purple silk sari sought her out. A conversation went on for several minutes, and then the woman's expression changed and she suddenly walked away. I noticed the abruptness of her leaving.
>
> "What happened, Mother?" I inquired.
>
> "We had a good conversation about India and the Sisters," said Mother Teresa.
>
> "She asked me about the work of the Sisters. I told her about Shishu Bhavan and the other work and then I began to tell her about our work for the lepers. She asked me if I worked with lepers myself. I said 'Yes,' and she left me. You must expect that when you work with lepers."
>
> "Did she say good-bye?" I asked. Mother Teresa smiled a bit ruefully and shook her head in the negative.

* * * * *

Even before 1965, the Missionaries of Charity had gone outside of Calcutta to other cities in India: Delhi, Jhansi, Agra, Asansol, Ambala, Bhagalpur, Patna, Darjeeling, Trivandrum. However, they had not yet gone beyond the borders of India. That became a possibility on February 1, 1965, five years after Mother Teresa's meeting with Cardinal Agagianian in Rome. It was on that date that she received the document in which the Holy See granted the *decretum laudis* to the Missionaries of Charity and raised the Congregation to a religious institute of pontifical right. Now Mother Teresa could establish houses outside of India, and she began by going with four Sisters to open a house in Cocorote, a remote village in Venezuela. That was on July 26, 1965. She had been invited there by Bishop Benitez of the diocese of Barquisimeto. He had heard about Mother Teresa at the Second Vatican Council. Thus, India, which for centuries had received missionaries from Spain, Portugal, France, Germany, Italy and Ireland, now sent out its first missionaries to a foreign country. The four Sisters who went to Venezuela were all Indian; they were the pioneer scouts of the Missionaries of Charity.

Mother Teresa once wrote: "You can find Calcutta in every part of the world, if you have eyes to see; wherever there are persons who are not loved, not wanted, not cared for — the rejected and the forgotten. This is the greatest poverty." Consequently, in her mind there are no limits or boundaries to the work of the Missionaries of Charity. "If there were poor people on the moon, we would have to go there."

Whenever Mother Teresa opens a house in any part of the world, she places only two conditions: the local bishop must send her a specific request, and her Sisters must be able to do a work that is not already being done by another religious institute. For example, the first house opened in Rome was at the request of the Bishop of Rome, Pope Paul VI. He had seen the work of the Missionaries of Charity during his pastoral visit to India in 1964. But before accepting the invitation, Mother Teresa made sure that of all the numerous religious institutes in Rome, there were none that worked among the poorest of the poor. She arrived in Rome with five Sisters on August 22, 1968, the feast of the Immaculate Heart of Mary, and opened a house in the slums of Tor Fiscale. It was the first foundation of the Sisters in Europe and was nothing but a barracks-like shanty with a roof of corrugated metal.

* * * * *

I have seen many houses of the Missionaries of Charity, and the furnishings are all more or less the same: second-hand furniture, tin plates, iron cots. The chapels are also the same: no pews, a small altar, and a crucifix with the usual placard, "I thirst." There is, however, a great difference in the localities in which the Missionaries of Charity serve the poorest of the poor. There is, for example, at Kalighat in Calcutta a home for the dying; in Rome, a house for transients inside the Vatican Walls; in New York City, a house for persons suffering from AIDS. In the walls of Vatican City an archway opens out on Porta Cavalleggeri, about 20 meters from the entrance to the Holy Office. The name-plate says *Casa Dono di Maria* (Gift of Mary House). Frequently I have found myself waiting at the traffic light on Porta Cavalleggeri. It is one of the slowest lights in Rome because it regulates the traffic for five streets that intersect at that point. Hence, I had plenty of time to observe the people who entered and departed through the archway. Many times I saw a tall, bent woman come out to empty a pail of garbage into the containers in front of the entrance. One afternoon two Missionaries of Charity, with their saris billowing in the breeze, knocked on the door with the palms of their hands, but no one answered. Evidently, the Sisters inside were busy. One evening, around six o'clock, a line of men formed in front of the closed door in the hope of receiving a meal. Most of the men were young, and the ethnic composition of the group was indicative of the latest wave of immigrants into Italy. Moroccans, Algerians, Polish, Albanians and Africans have come to eat at the table of the *Casa Dono di Maria*. There is also a permanent residence available for the transients of Rome. There are 72 beds for the vagrants, some of whom have been stranded due to the closing of mental institutions, while others are alcoholics or the aged poor who are all alone.

Mother Teresa opened the house in the Vatican wall on May 18, 1987. She explained: "It is the result of a desire that originated with Pope John Paul II during his pastoral visit to Calcutta. I have never had any difficulty with the Vatican bureaucracy. It was always enough to say: 'The Holy Father wants it,' and everything went smoothly."

In New York, at 657 Washington Street, the name-plate says: "Missionaries of Charity." The house is called "Gift of Love," and it is a residence for people suffering from AIDS. Mother Teresa opened it in 1985 at the request of Cardinal John J. O'Connor, Archbishop of New York. It is a four-story building with a chapel, and above the chapel door is a list of the names of those who have died. The first name on the list is Raymond Galvin, who died on December 10, 1985. Visitors are not permitted on the floors, out of respect for the sick, who do not want to be objects of curiosity. The first patients were selected by Mother Teresa out of the prisons, where they would not have completed their sentences because they were dying of AIDS. Mother Teresa tells the following story about one of the patients: "After he had been with us for some time, he confided to me: 'Mother, when I get a headache, I share it with Jesus crowned with thorns; when I have pains in my back, I share them with Jesus scourged at the pillar; when my hands and feet hurt, I share it with Jesus nailed to the cross.' ... And this man, only a few months before, was in prison for life because of some terrible crime."

THE COMMANDOS

Mother Teresa is not only a specialist in the diseases of the world, she is also quick to offer help in times of disaster: earthquakes, floods and the horrors of war. She takes off at once, in spite of bureaucratic obstacles, conflicting opinions, bombed airports, risks and dangers. As soon as she arrives on the scene, she sizes up the situation and quickly organizes the Sisters and volunteers. They are transformed into "commandos," wearing the blue helmets of first-aid workers. I have met some who have returned from the scene of a disaster. I want to give a summary of the testimony that I have collected through the years. It is very diverse, and yet it is all the same.

* * * * *

In December of 1979 I was writing an article about the awarding of the Nobel Peace Prize to Mother Teresa, when an old friend, a Salesian missionary named Father Silvano Garrello, came into the office.

"Am I disturbing you?" he asked.

"Of course you're disturbing me," I replied. "I'm writing an article on Mother Teresa."

"Now don't forget that Mother Teresa is a saint, surely, but she is also a great administrator. I can assure you of that because I have seen her in action."

Then, without waiting to be asked, Father Silvano sat down and told me the following story.

"I was in Calcutta in December of 1971, a time of chaos and havoc. It was during the war with Bangladesh and there were ten million refugees awaiting the relief that was late in coming. Each day we had reports of massacres and indescribable suffering. I attended a meeting of representatives of various charitable organizations from India, Italy, the United States and Switzerland. We were trying to reach agreement on how to arrange the re-entry of the refugees into Bengal. We discussed the matter for several hours, trying to solve all kinds of problems: where we would get trucks, how we could provide kitchens and hospital tents, how we should set up the refugee camps. Then Mother Teresa, the specialist, entered the discussion. She spoke for only two minutes and summed up everything in a few words. Immediately everything became clear; the relief supplies were prepared and the roads were opened. The head of a multinational relief organization turned and stared with astonishment at her efficiency.

"The war with Bangladesh ended on December 16, leaving behind the usual effects of war. Approximately 200,000 girls had been violated by the soldiers. Many of them committed suicide; many others were left pregnant. The official policy was to perform abortions, but Mother Teresa opposed this and sent her Sisters into action. In less than 20 days, by the beginning of January, 1972, she had established a center for the girls at Dacca, with a delivery room and a nursery for the newborn infants."

Later on, Mother Teresa herself wrote about the raped girls of Bangladesh: "We were faced with a very serious problem because it was against the law of the Muslims and the Hindus to receive back into the family or into civil society girls who had been violated.... I said to them: 'Our girls have been taken by force; they did not intend to sin. But what you plan to do or what you want to help them to do, that *is* a sin, and it will haunt them for the rest of their lives. They will not be able to forget that they are mothers who have caused the death of their own babies.'

"Thanks be to God, the government of Bangladesh understood that I was willing to take care of the babies. So it was established by law that only if a girl voluntarily decided to have an abortion would the doctors be permitted to touch her."

Father Silvano described another incident that occurred during that tragic December of 1971: "Mother Teresa prevented the massacre of the *bihari*, the Indian soldiers of Bihar who had aided the Pakistani troops. At the end of the war the *bihari* were looked upon as enemies of the recently proclaimed independent state of Bangladesh. They were dragged from their hide-outs, tortured, and then stood against the wall. I still can't understand how she did it, but somehow she managed to gather the soldiers together in protected camps and thus save them from certain death. An army general could not have better organized the rescue of the retreating troops."

* * * * *

In the courtyard of the papal summer residence at Castel Gandolfo, Pope John Paul II was addressing a group of young people from the "Giorgio La Pira" youth movement. It was August 9, 1982, a very hot and sultry day. On the way to the papal palace, we stopped and lined up at the fountain in the piazza to refresh ourselves. Bishop Dante Bernini of Albano, the president of the Justice and Peace Commission, had just finished speaking when Mother Teresa emerged from the shadows on the balcony of the papal residence. Pope John Paul immediately arose and went to meet her. Then, taking her by the hand, he led her to a chair next to his, and turning to the crowd in the courtyard below, he said: "Mother Teresa has come to ask for a few words and a blessing because tomorrow she leaves for Beirut." It was evident that she was going as the "vicar" of the

Pope on a journey that he could not make, but which he had been thinking of since June.

The Pope than began a dialogue with the young people, questions and answers. One of them asked: "How can the Church speak of the problems in Lebanon in the Gospel language of Christians?" Pope John Paul replied: "Mother Teresa, who is going to Lebanon, knows how to do that without having studied many books. She knows because that language comes from her soul, her charism, her heart." Without having studied it in books and being unschooled in politics and the art of diplomacy, Mother Teresa departed for the inferno of Lebanon. In the following days the newspapers carried accounts of her visit. In her book, *Such a Vision of the Street*, Eileen Egan describes that trip:

> To reach her Sisters in Beirut, long a cauldron of violence, she took a plane from Rome to Athens and then another plane to Cyprus. From Cyprus, the only means of reaching Beirut was a seventeen-hour boat trip. She found the six Sisters safe in Mar Takla, in East Beirut. John de Salis, head of the Red Cross delegation in Lebanon, told Mother Teresa of the plight of mentally ill children in an asylum of the upper floor of Dar al-Ajaza Islamia, a home for the aged. The home, located near a camp of Palestinian refugees, had been damaged by bombs. The needs of the children for food, water and adequate shelter were tragically acute. Mother Teresa decided that all the children could be housed with her Sisters who had already opened a refuge for the homeless and destitute. The problem was that Dar al-Ajaza was situated across the Green Line, the no-man's land separating the predominantly Muslim sector from East Beirut, home of the Christian Lebanese. Mother Teresa insisted on crossing the line to evacuate the

children. Against the advice even of church leaders, Mother Teresa travelled with four Red Cross vehicles into war-ravaged West Beirut to rescue the children.

They found thirty-seven children, from seven to twenty-one, the most helpless examples of humanity. Among them were the deformed, the paralyzed, the severely mentally retarded, youngsters unaware of what was happening around them, but able to suffer hunger, thirst and fear. Mother Teresa went among them, embracing them and giving a handshake to the older children. Among the Muslim children were some Palestinians. One by one, Mother Teresa, the International Red Cross and the volunteers packed up the children and carried or led them to the ve- hicles. The convoy crossed the Green Line at the Israeli-controlled checkpoint and rushed them to the Mar Takla convent. Two days later, Mother Teresa crossed the Green Line again to evacuate another twenty-seven children.

One of the Red Cross officials commented: "What stunned everyone was her energy. She saw the prob- lem, fell to her knees and prayed for a few seconds, and then she was rattling off a list of supplies she needed.... We didn't expect a saint to be so efficient."

* * * * *

Father Leo Maasburg was preparing for the celebration of Christmas when he received a fax from Moscow. It was dated December 22, 1988, and said: "Father Leo: Come immediately. Bring everything. God bless you. Mother Teresa."

"If I leave at once," thought Father Leo, "I'll be back by Christmas; maybe even for Christmas Eve." He thought it would be a mission of only a few days, but he did not yet know that Mother Teresa was planning for him to minister to the

Sisters and the victims of the earthquake in Armenia. He would spend six months in the Soviet Union.

Father Maasburg is Austrian. He had been practicing law in Vienna and became a priest at the age of 33. "God called me at the right moment," he said. He now lives in Rome and has accompanied Mother Teresa on many journeys.

The fax did not contain an invitation, but a command. What power does Mother Teresa have that she can command obedience?

"One can achieve much by human power, manipulation or force, but Mother Teresa does not wield power in a human sense, although she has a strong and forceful personality. I would describe her secret as a kind of divine wisdom. God does not force; he offers. Mother Teresa touches the very core of a person, and as for me, she has always been able to elicit from me an immediate 'yes.'

"I forgot about my priestly duties in Rome, my scheduled appointments, important meetings, and even my promise to my household that I would spend Christmas at home. Mother Teresa is able to sweep away all the objections that can be put forth in the name of convenience, prestige, profit and good manners. She can touch a heart of stone and transform it into a heart of flesh and blood."

That was in 1988, when Mother Teresa had gone to the Soviet Union after the earthquake of December 7 in Armenia, the smallest of the eighteen republics of the former USSR, now dissolved since the events of December 1991. The quake measured nine points (out of a possible twelve based on the amount of destruction caused) on the Mercalli scale and its epicenter was between Tblisi, the capital of Georgia, and Erevan, the capital of Armenia. It had destroyed buildings of reinforced concrete at Leninaken, the second largest city in Armenia; at Kirovaken, the third largest city; and it had demolished cities such as Spitak. The official statistics estimated thousands dead, tens of thousands injured, and a half million homeless.

Relief was delayed for a long time, due to chaotic disorganization, the harsh winter weather, and the impassable roads that made the remote villages inaccessible. The little Armenian nation had suffered persecutions throughout the centuries. It lived through the tragedy of the genocide inflicted by the Turks in 1915 and the desperate revolt against the people of Azerbaijan. Now it had suffered another disaster of such magnitude that it seemed to surpass all human endurance. The thousands of dead had found peace at last; the survivors were living in tents, huddled around fires against the sub-zero weather. Mother Teresa arrived with her "commandos": the Yugoslav, Sister Stanislava; the Indian, Sister Placida; the Italian, Sister Giacinta, together with Father Leo Maasburg, whom she had summoned from Rome. But what relief could they bring to that sea of despair?

* * * * *

Father Leo had arrived in Moscow by Aeroflot, in the morning, bringing 40 boxes of clothing, blankets and candles. Mother Teresa was waiting for him at the airport in order to resolve any possible difficulties with the customs. She took charge of everything, counting the boxes to make sure that every box passed through customs. They then proceeded to a hospital in government vehicles, where three rooms had been allotted for her use.

The first room, which had been used for physical therapy, was made into a chapel, containing a table for an altar, a portable tabernacle, and a statue of Our Lady of Fatima, which Mother Teresa had brought with her. During the flight from Calcutta, speaking to a stewardess, she referred to the statue as "the passenger in my arms." Father Leo celebrated Christmas midnight Mass in the chapel, and on Christmas day they departed for Erevan.

On that Christmas day in 1988 the airport in Moscow was

snowed in. Mother Teresa did not want to go back to the city, fearing that she would miss the plane that sooner or later would be able to land. She waited with Father Leo and the Sisters in a room provided for her by the director of the airport. Mother Teresa was sitting under a portrait of Lenin, with a basket of apples and oranges at her side. As she waited, she browsed through a copy of the newspaper, *Pravda*, prayed the rosary, or spoke in soft tones to the other Sisters. That is the way Mother Teresa spent the day, and when the plane finally landed, six hours late, they had to wait yet another four hours before the plane could take off again.

It was dark when the group arrived at Erevan. The streets were deserted because of the curfew. Most of the houses in the city had collapsed and the soldiers had gathered the survivors in the city stadium. A car from the Committee for Peace collected the Sisters and the priest and took them to the children's hospital. But the day was not yet over for Mother Teresa and she showed no signs of weariness. She wanted to inspect the place and, still standing, she made her decisions: this will be the chapel, this will be the refectory, this will be the dormitory. Father Leo experienced a bit of anxiety when they showed him the room assigned to him: no heat, pipes for hot water, but no hot water. Only one's breath could give a bit of warmth to the tiny room. It had been transformed into a bedroom and the only furnishings were a cot and a white plastic chair. His anxiety vanished, however, when Mother Teresa entered the room. She looked around and then said: "A beautiful sacrifice, eh?" She said this with such an easy, carefree look that Father Leo broke out in a burst of nervous laughter. The temperature outside was more than 60 degrees below zero. Father Leo's luggage had been lost at some point in the journey, and all he had was his hand luggage, his overcoat, and his galoshes. But Mother Teresa's short visit changed his mood. No use crying over the lost luggage; he was grateful to have the carry-on luggage.

"Mother Teresa spent four days in Erevan, and when she

left, she gave us our instructions. Her first words were: 'Do humble work. Give witness with gentleness and joy. Be humble like Mary and holy like Jesus.'

"During the first few days I felt that I would have very little to do as chaplain, but in a short time I was kept very busy. We had 600 children in the hospital and many of them had lost their parents in the earthquake. The Sisters could not speak Armenian; they were simply there, with the children. They could not communicate in words, but by means of signs, smiles, tenderness and prayer, their communication was very effective. The children had never seen Sisters because there were none in Armenia. They knew only the word 'Catholic' and the head of the Armenian church. The Sisters carried out the instructions of Mother Teresa: to give witness to the love of Jesus."

"Were they also supposed to make converts?"

"No, Mother Teresa has said repeatedly that her mission is not to make converts but simply to give witness to the love of Jesus through love of neighbor. She gives a sign; then each one chooses as he or she wishes. This is her rule. She is not a missionary in the traditional sense of converting and baptizing. She reminds me of the famous saying of St. Paul when he had to deal with the discord and division in the church at Corinth: 'Thank God I baptized none of you except Crispus and Gaius, so there are none who can say that you were baptized in my name.... For Christ did not send me to baptize, but to preach the gospel — not with wordy "wisdom," however, lest the cross of Christ be rendered void of its meaning.' This is also the method of Mother Teresa and the Missionaries of Charity."

* * * * *

The way the Soviet authorities treated Mother Teresa was most unusual. She was warmly received, rooms were provided for her in the various hospitals, automobiles awaited her at the airports. She was granted many privileges and received help on all sides. When she first visited the Soviet Union, there was no freedom of religion. Lenin had written in 1922: "We must commit ourselves to a definitive battle against the reactionary clergy and annihilate the resistance of priests and monks with such cruelty that they will remember it for decades to come."

That battle against religion did not end until April of 1990, and in September of that year, for the first time since 1918, the Eucharistic liturgy was celebrated in the Cathedral of the Assumption within the walls of the Kremlin. After the liturgy, Alexis II, the Patriarch of all Russia, led the first procession in 70 years from the Kremlin to the Church of the Ascension, which had been restored after being used for half a century as a storehouse for potatoes. Freedom of conscience became a law of the State by a vote of the Soviet Parliament: 341 in favor and 2 opposed. But none of this had yet occurred in 1988, so who opened the doors of the Soviet Union to Mother Teresa?

Father Leo answers the question this way: "I don't believe that very much was known about Mother Teresa in the Soviet Union until a documentary about her and the Missionaries of Charity was shown at a TV film festival that was held in Moscow in July of 1987. The film was produced by Ann and Jeannette Petrie. Mother Teresa was immediately invited officially to visit Moscow and she made her first visit on August 19, 1988. After that, things moved rapidly. On December 8, the feast of the Immaculate Conception, she received permission to send five Missionaries of Charity to a hospital for handicapped children in Moscow. Consequently, when she arrived in Moscow shortly after the earthquake in Armenia, she already had many friends and numerous sources of help there."

"How was she received by the people of Erevan in Armenia?"

"There were many who recognized Mother Teresa because they had seen her on Soviet television. The nurses in the hospital vied with one another to have their pictures taken with her; on the street the people greeted her and gladly accepted the religious medals that she handed out to them. As regards myself, it was at the request of Mother Teresa that I was invited by the Soviet authorities to take part in the relief work for the victims of the earthquake. A foreign priest had not received an official invitation in 70 years. The Sisters were appreciated immediately because of their humility, their smiles and their availability. In the midst of all that suffering, we were received with affection. They brought us flowers and little gifts and even food, which it was hard to accept because we knew that they were taking it out of their own mouths."

"The Sisters took care of the children in the hospital, and what did you do, Father Leo?"

"My duty was to help and to give spiritual aid to those poor people who had lost everything. In spite of the persecutions of the past, the Armenians have preserved in their hearts a simple but profound faith. In their suffering their faith came to the surface, and I have very moving proof of that. One day in a village I met a civil engineer who asked me to bless his daughter. I entered his temporary shelter of corrugated metal, the kind used on construction sites. It was very special because all the other people were living in tents. The hut was empty, so I asked where the little girl was. He showed me a package containing the remains of calcified bones and a piece of cloth that had been scorched by fire. His young daughter had died in the house three months ago, when it was destroyed by fire at the time of the earthquake. I was overcome with horror and with compassion.

"The engineer hastened to fetch his wife, and then we all knelt down and prayed together. They wept all the time that I was there. I blessed the remains and suggested that they should be buried. I promised that I would celebrate a Mass for them, and on the specified day they got up at three o'clock in the morning to get to Erevan for the six o'clock Mass.

"Some weeks later, as I was passing through the same

village, the engineer came running toward me. 'Thank you, thank you,' he shouted. 'We are at peace now.' Once again the Lord had healed a deep wound."

On her return from Armenia, Mother Teresa stopped at Rome. I asked how her Christmas was among the victims of the earthquake, and she answered: "Mary and Joseph looked for a place where Jesus could be born. They found it in Armenia. Jesus was born in poverty; he had nothing but hay and a stable. The poverty of Christ and the suffering of the Armenian people are united. Armenia was Golgotha — death; but then it became Bethlehem and the world hastened to it, as the shepherds and the Three Kings had done."

THE POOR RICH

The office of Gjon Sinishta, administrator at the University of San Francisco, is the epitome of comfort: air conditioned, plush carpeting, sturdy furniture, and a discreet secretary who served coffee and then left. It seems more out of place to talk about Mother Teresa here than in any other place in this affluent American society. In India, when Mother Teresa says "the poorest of the poor," one knows exactly what she means. But in California, where good health is obligatory, beauty is a cult, and wealth is a Calvinistic sign of divine benevolence, Mother Teresa could be considered an eccentric old woman, exotically dressed like a "hippy," who travels around carrying a shopping bag, like the homeless "bag ladies" who live on the street — a transient. Perhaps that is the way some generous Catholics in San Francisco thought of her on a day that they found her behavior irritating to the point of being offensive. They complained to the archbishop: "Why is that Indian nun permitted to lecture to us?" The "Indian nun" had challenged the American way of life, as traditional as apple pie and as sacred as the article in the Constitution that guarantees every citizen's right to life, liberty and the pursuit of happiness.

That is the story that Gjon Sinishta told me, and not without some amusement. Gjon Sinishta, 62 years old, is an Albanian refugee who has lived in the United States since 1965. In Albania he studied under the Jesuits in Scutari, but the school was closed by the anti-religious regime. The students were dispersed and the rector and the professors were imprisoned. In 1949 Gjon became a member of the Communist party and was hired as a journalist by a radio station in Belgrade. "I lived two lives," he said. "I had the faith in my heart and a Communist membership card in my pocket. I was in danger of abandoning my religion, so in 1956 I tried to escape to the free world. I was just a few feet from the border when the dogs of the frontier guards caught up with me. After the trial I was sentenced to five years and five months in prison for espionage."

While serving his sentence in the Sremska Mitrovica prison, he worked in the factory, making wheels for automobiles. His quota was 135 wheels a day, and if he did not meet that quota, he was deprived of bread and soup. "Under those circumstances a man who did not have the faith or an ideal became a number, an animal, or a spy for the guards." When he finished his prison term, Gjon escaped to Austria, hidden in a truck. In 1964 he emigrated to the United States, where he found work in college administration, first at the University of Detroit and then at the University of San Francisco, both Jesuit universities. He founded the ACIC, the Albanian Center of Catholic Information. Its purpose is to aid the Church in Albania and to denounce the violation of human rights. After religious liberty was granted in Albania, the Center began working for the restoration of churches and ecclesiastical properties that had been confiscated by the government and checking to see that religious freedom actually exists. He has also founded an association of Albanians living in the United States; it has 200,000 members, most of whom work in restaurants and factories in various cities such as New York, Boston, Cleveland, Detroit, Chicago and Los Angeles.

* * * * *

Gjon Sinishta gave the following account of the arrival of the Missionaries of Charity in San Francisco: "Mother Teresa wanted to open a central novitiate in the United States for the formation of new members of the Missionaries of Charity. Archbishop John Quinn of San Francisco offered her a parish convent that was no longer in use. On the day that Mother Teresa was to arrive, the Archbishop asked me to accompany him to the airport. 'Greet her in Albanian,' he said. 'That will be a nice surprise.'

"The plane arrived at 8:30 in the evening and the weather was foggy and chilly. Our group was waiting in a private room: Archbishop Quinn, the Consul General of India, the editor of *The San Francisco Catholic*, and myself. When Mother Teresa arrived, I greeted her in Albanian: *'Nana Tereza, kioft levdue Jezu Krishti e mirese keni ardhe ne San Francisco!'* (Mother Teresa, praised be Jesus Christ and welcome to San Francisco!). She jerked back and opened her eyes wide. She asked: *'Po ju jeni shqiptar?'* (Are you Albanian?). We embraced and I felt deeply moved by her presence. It was like being near something sacred, and I was struck by her simplicity.

"The next day more than 5,000 people gathered in the cathedral to see Mother Teresa. The Archbishop then took her to St. Paul's parish to turn the house over to her. As I said, it was a convent that had long been unused, but the parishioners had been generous in donating toward its renewal. The rooms had been newly painted; the floor was covered with pearl gray carpeting; in the dining room there were electric machines for making coffee, toast and for squeezing orange juice; there were two refrigerators in the kitchen, a television set in the parlor, and an air conditioner in each room. In the chapel there were new pews and there was carpeting on the floor. In a word, the parishioners had provided all the comforts of a typical American convent. They were rightly proud of the work that had been done with their donations.

"When Mother Teresa entered the building, the smile

faded from her face. She looked around at everything in silence, but frowning more and more. Then, without asking the Archbishop, she commanded the Sisters and volunteers who had accompanied her to take everything out. We were all dumbfounded. We saw them roll up the carpets and pick up the rugs; then they took down the venetian blinds from the windows. All the electrical appliances were taken outside. 'Whoever wants them can take them,' said Mother Teresa. The pews were removed from the chapel and carried into the church yard. After several hours of work, there remained only the cots in the bedrooms, the table and chairs on the bare floor of the dining room, and the gas stove in the kitchen."

The two sisters, Ann and Jeannette Petrie, were present because they were accompanying Mother Teresa and making a documentary for TV. They filmed the entire incredible incident: the rolled-up carpets and rugs being carried out of the house, together with the new pews from the chapel; the removal of the venetian blinds from the windows as well as the air conditioners; the systematic stripping of the house of all the electric appliances that are the pride of American technology. When it was all done, Mother Teresa spoke into the microphone of Ann and Jeannette and explained what had happened:

> Many persons do not understand why we do not use washing machines and refrigerators, why we do not listen to the radio, why we do not watch television, why we do not go to the movies or accept invitations to social functions. They are natural things and there is nothing evil in them. But as far as we are concerned, we have decided not to use them. In order to understand the poor, we ought to know what poverty is. We do not accept any government assistance or church subsidies, salaries or fixed income. The birds of the air and the flowers of the field do not have an income, but God takes care of them. Therefore, will not God also

take care of us, who are more important than flowers and birds?

Gjon Sinishta continued his description of the incident: "There was general consternation and in the following days some persons went to complain to the Archbishop. 'We are in America,' they said, 'not in India.' Even some of the priests and local Sisters were indignant. Some even criticized the Archbishop for not knowing in advance the lifestyle of the Missionaries of Charity.

"The following Sunday, in the chapel without pews or carpeting, the people had to kneel on the bare floor. Some of them had come precisely to complain to Mother Teresa for her lack of gratitude. Even the Archbishop had seemed to be somewhat annoyed. At the end of the Mass Mother Teresa rose to speak. She did not try to justify her actions nor did she ask pardon. She said simply: "To be accepted by the poor, we must live like the poor. Poverty is our charism. I entrust my Sisters to you; do not spoil them. Help them to observe poverty. We do not simply endure poverty, but we choose it voluntarily for the love of Jesus and the poor."

* * * * *

Some time later, Mother Teresa was interviewed for *Time* magazine. The journalist, Edward W. Desmond, asked her: "Is the materialism of the West a serious problem?"

Anyone who does not understand the basic philosophy of Mother Teresa may think that her response was a stern reprimand: "I don't know. That doesn't concern me; I have to think about so many other things. We do not possess anything, and therefore we are not preoccupied with anything. The more you possess, the more you are preoccupied; the less you possess, the freer you are. For us, poverty means freedom. It is not a mortification or a penance; it is a joyful freedom. Look, there is no television here; there is neither this nor that. Although it gets very hot here, in the whole house there is only one fan, and that is not for us but for the guests. Nevertheless, we are perfectly happy."

The journalist pursued the matter: "But you have been sharply criticized for the severity of life that you impose on yourself and your Sisters."

Mother Teresa's answer was quick in coming: "We have freely chosen that, and this is the difference between us and the poor. How could they believe in us if our life were any different? If we had everything that money can buy, that the world can give, how could they relate to us? What language could I use with them? But now, if someone were to say to me: 'I'm dying of the heat today,' I could respond: 'Come and see how hot it is in my room'."

The journalist was a bit moved by this and he asked: "Mother Teresa, what do you think of the rich?"

"I think that the rich are the poorest of the poor, because very often they are never content; they always want something more. I don't say that they are all like that; no one is exactly the same as anyone else.... It is difficult to control that tendency; it is also more difficult to satisfy the hunger for love than the hunger for bread."

* * * * *

Having made peace with the parishioners after her little speech in the chapel, Mother Teresa now returns to San Francisco each year in May to receive the religious profession of the novices. Usually there are as many as 60 novices in the novitiate. Archbishop Quinn has invited Mother Teresa to open another house on Fulton Street, near the University, for those suffering from AIDS. The superior of the house is Sister Sylvia, and Gjon Sinishta has organized a group of student volunteers to help the Sisters care for the sick. The group is under the direction of Steve

Bosque, a sturdily built youth who is very energetic and available.

Steve told me: "We do not speak about death to the patients, but about football and current events, about trust in God and the consolation that it brings. There is always another day, and if a person does not have that trust, he just lets himself go. Those patients have experienced abandonment and marginalization. The Sisters treat them like human beings. They are more than nurses; they are friends who stop to chat with the patients for hours at a time. We volunteers try to follow their example."

There is another scene in the TV documentary made by Ann and Jeannette Petrie. It shows Mother Teresa speaking to a group of novices. They are all very young, and the majority of them have the dark complexion of Indians, but mixed in with them are the white faces of American and European novices. They are dressed in the white sari, but without the blue border, which they will wear after their final profession. Mother Teresa says to them: "I want to tell you something important. None of us has come here simply to increase our number. We have much work to do, but I am not interested in numbers. None of you has entered this Congregation to be a number. Each one of you has come in order to be a Missionary of Charity, to make a career out of the love of God. And each one of you is unique. If we do not feel impelled to help the poor, it is better that we pack up and go home. Return home, because there is no use in remaining here."

THE SMILE OF GOD

N adir Panda, the pilot of the Air India jumbo jet, lands the plane at Fiumicino Airport in Rome at 4:20 in the afternoon, and ten minutes later the plane draws up to Gate 8. Flight AI/155 is six hours late and the pilot is very annoyed. So also is the agent of the airline who is waiting in a car at the gate. That particular flight, which normally is scheduled to land at Fiumicino at 10:30 in the morning each day, would on this particular day, April 25, 1990, be a mark against a company that, like all airlines, spends millions of dollars each year to advertise its efficient service. Tomorrow the daily papers will carry the news that Mother Teresa arrived in Rome, with the inevitable comment: "six hours late."

"Technical reasons," says the representative of Air India in Rome. At the office of the airline at Fiumicino the journalists, who have been waiting since early morning, receive an even more vague explanation.

"It's due to operational problems that arise during transit. There are so many stops — Bombay, Calcutta, Delhi, Frankfurt, Rome — that on such a long flight delays are always possible."

Mother Teresa appears at the door of the economy class, holding a child by the hand. Behind her is a Sister with a small child in her arms. Mother Teresa descends with rapid steps and walks with bowed head toward the automobile provided for her by Air India. Fluffy white clouds are floating in the sky and the air is brightly illumined by the light of a Roman afternoon in the springtime. Mother Teresa stops for a moment and lifts up her head; a smile breaks out on her wrinkled face. At last, she is in Rome. She has returned after an absence of eight months — eight months spent in Calcutta, where she was hospitalized and then had to endure a long period of convalescence. In September of 1989 newspapers around the world had published the news of her heart attack. In the more sensational papers the headline stated: "Mother Teresa between life and death." In March the headlines were based on a statement she had made: "I hope that my last journey will be to heaven." In April came the news of her resignation as superior general of the Missionaries of Charity: "Sick and exhausted, Teresa of Calcutta resigns." But here she is in Rome, a bit smaller and more stooped perhaps, but her step is still lively and her bearing resolute. Tomorrow the headlines will read: "Mother Teresa is in Rome and is well."

* * * * *

Settled in her seat in economy class, Mother Teresa passed the hours of the interminable journey with her eyes closed and her rosary in her hands. She did not eat the breakfast or the lunch served on the plane, but she took the envelopes of sugar, salt and powdered milk, as well as the small containers of jelly, and placed them in her shopping bag. She always does that. She comes from a place where the children fight with the rats for food, and a few ounces of sugar can prolong for a day the life of an old person who is dying from hunger.

In the small crowd at the airport a man remains glued to the glass door of the section for international arrivals; a woman sits motionless and expectant in the waiting room. They are Mr. Leocaldi and Mrs. Pini. They are waiting for the Sister from Calcutta who will deliver to each of them a long-desired child.

When Mother Teresa exits from customs, Mr. Leocaldi rushes toward her and Mrs. Pini rises from her seat, but their advance is blocked by the pushing and shoving of the journalists and photographers. The baby, Sweety, thirteen months old, is passed immediately to the arms of Mr. Leocaldi, but Montu, three and a half years old, is still walking at the side of Mother Teresa. When Mrs. Pini is finally able to reach Mother Teresa, Montu lets himself be lifted in her arms but looks around to try and see Mother Teresa, who notices that last look and hesitates for a moment before she is carried along by the crowd.

Sweety and Montu will change their names and their nationality. They will drink homogenized milk instead of eating boiled rice. One of them will learn to speak Italian with a Neapolitan accent and the other with a Tuscan accent. Like all the adopted children, they will have four parents: two by blood and two by the heart. The adopting parents, Mr. and Mrs. Pini and Mr. and Mrs. Leocaldi, will tell their adopted child: "Mother Teresa brought you, and when she gave you to us, she said: 'I entrust to you the smile of God'."

* * * * *

In the house of the Missionaries of Charity at San Gregorio al Celio in Rome, there is a parlor set aside for couples who are asking to adopt a child. Many couples have come here after alternating between hope and despair, due to the bureaucracy of the courts and the legal obstacles to these special cases of adoption. While waiting to speak with Sister Prema, who is in charge of adoption procedures, they look at the posters on the wall. One of them is a map of the world published by the *National Geographic*. Under the map is a printed statement that Mother Teresa often repeats: "Rejoice because once again Christ walks through the world doing good in you and through you." On a bulletin board there are photos of children, most of them Indian, who have been given out for adoption. They range in ages from one month to ten years. The photos are arranged around a picture frame containing a typewritten copy of "The Story of an Adopted Child":

> There were two women who never knew each other.
> One you do not remember; the other you call Mama.
> The first one gave you life;
> The second one taught you to live it.
> The first one created in you a need for love;
> The second one was there to satisfy that need.
> One of them gave you your nationality;
> The other one gave you your name.
> One of them gave you the seed for growth;
> The other gave you a goal.
> One of them provided you with emotions;
> The other calmed your fears.
> One of them saw your first smile;
> The other wiped away your tears.
> One of them left you; it was all she could do;
> The other prayed for a child, and the Lord led her
>   to you.
> And now you ask me the inevitable question:
> What molded me, heredity or environment?
> Neither the one nor the other, but only two
>   different loves.

* * * * *

It is the first Sunday in May and Mother Teresa has been in Rome for a week. She is waiting for two couples, the Croce's from the Province of Firenze, and the Forzini's from Siena. To each couple she had given two children some years ago. She is anxious, and every now and then she looks out the door, wondering why they are so late. When the two families finally arrive, Mother Teresa acts like a grandmother who has not seen her grandchildren for a long time. She raises her arms and claps her hands together, uttering short phrases of wonderment: "How you have grown! How tall you are! How good you look!"

She pats the children on the head and hugs them tightly. Then, turning to the two couples, she says gratefully: "These children would have been aborted if it had not been for you. Thank you, thank you!"

"May you live for a long time, Mother," says one of the parents.

Raising her eyes, Mother responds: "As long as God wants."

"The first time we met Mother Teresa and told her we wanted a child," says Maria Luisa Croce," she said, "'Thank you.' Do you understand? She thanked *us*! That opened a new world to us. Previously we had dealt only with social workers, who treated us as if we were beggars asking for alms when we inquired about adopting a child. They took advantage of the psychological situation, telling us that there are too many couples asking for children, that there are few children available, and finally that it is all a bargaining process and sometimes, unfortunately, amounts to trafficking in children. With Mother Teresa, however, the procedure is simple and joyful. Our desire to raise a child coincides with her desire to save a child that would otherwise have been aborted or, if delivered, immediately abandoned."

Maria Luisa and Massimo Croce are both teachers; she an instructor on child care and he a professor of geometry. They had first adopted Shana, an infant eleven months old, and later Vikas, seven and a half years old. Shana had arrived at Fiumicino Airport on July 26, 1986, in the arms of a Missionary of Charity. Maria Luisa had been so overcome with emotion that she had to be taken to the First Aid Station in the airport with heart palpitations.

"Sister Prema always laughs when we talk about that and she tells me: 'One goes to a hospital for a delivery, but you went to the First Aid Station.'

"Shana spent the first eleven months of her life with the Sisters at Shishu Bhavan, until July 26, 1986, when we went to the airport to receive her. Her arrival was almost like a normal birth; we saw our baby and immediately we were her parents. It's true that I was taken to the First Aid Station with heart palpitations. The mother was unprepared for that first 'delivery' and the emotion was overwhelming.

"In the case of Vikas it was more complicated. He arrived on September 9, 1989, and he was older. He was born at Takdah on March 19, 1982, and had lived for six years with his parents and a brother whom he loved very much. For that reason his memories of India are sweet and pleasant. His mother died in April of 1988 and his father, who was poor and ill, could no longer care for him. He gave Vikas to the Missionaries of Charity and signed the document of renunciation. Vikas never saw his father or brother again.

"Our relationship with Vikas has been more mature and challenging. He has learned to love us little by little, but he has always nourished the hope of returning to his family. We had to understand that he accepted us, but only for the time being. But later on, our love and God's love made us a happy family. We feel a little Indian, even though we have never been to India. The reason is that our children are Indian and we have been called to continue the work of their Indian parents. Some day, when Shana and Vikas are grown up, we'll go to India and perhaps find our roots."

* * * * *

Sandra and Lorenzo Forzini were married in 1972. She is a housewife and he is a radiologist. They had wanted to have a large family and had decided to adopt a child who could grow up with their own children. But they never had any children, so after years of waiting, medical consultations and useless medication, they turned to Luciano Grossi, the man in charge of

Mother Teresa's adoptions in Tuscany. After the prospective parents received a certificate of their fitness to adopt a child, Luciano Grossi made arrangements for them to meet Sister Prema in Rome. Ten months after their first meeting, they received from India a passport-size photo of a baby girl named Reshmi, which means "sunbeam." They immediately decided to call her Maria Reshmi.

"At that moment we had become parents at last; she was our daughter."

But other documents were requested, so they sent them to Calcutta and waited for the approval of the judge of the children's court in Calcutta in order to obtain the decree of adoption. "Another year passed," said Dr. Forzini, "and it seemed interminable. The approval could be granted at any moment, but Calcutta is far away and we had heard nothing. In August of 1983 we sent a telegram to the Missionaries of Charity to advise them that we were ready to go to India. In their reply they explained the reason for the long delay: the documents were being held up at the customs in Calcutta. They also advised us that the meeting in the juvenile court was scheduled for September 15.

"Finally we arrived at the orphanage Shishu Bhavan in Calcutta and the Sisters placed our baby in our arms. She was seventeen months old. However, it takes time; an adopted baby does not become a daughter as soon as she is held in one's arms. That happens gradually, and the progress is imperceptible.

"Four years later, in 1987, Mother Teresa gave us another baby. Her name was Manisha, which means "desire," and we had her baptized as Paola Manisha. We had also wanted this second child very much. Usually the Sisters discourage the adoption of a second child, and they are right, because there are so many couples waiting. At Shishu Bhavan most of the babies are girls because in India a male child is seldom abandoned. As soon as he is old enough, he can help support the family. But a girl child is considered a burden; she is not economically productive, and if she has no dowry she will not find a husband."

"Mrs. Forzini, how did you learn how to become parents?"

"We had to accept the children as they were, adjusting ourselves to their characters without trying to change them. It has been a long and difficult road, but an exciting one. Maria Reshmi is alert, decisive and strong, as the Sister had told us at the very beginning. At the age of one and a half she was very good with the other children. For example, she was smart enough to keep the gate closed so that the smaller ones would not fall down the stairs. She was immediately at ease with us, as she had been in the orphanage.

"Paola Manisha, on the other hand, had difficulty in adjusting. She didn't react to any stimulus and she refused everything. She was even afraid of the things that children usually like, such as toys and dogs. She clung to me for almost a year, seeking that physical rapport that she had never had. Once this tremendous need for an exclusive love for one person had been satisfied, a need that had kept her paralyzed, as it were, she began to be more outgoing and to relate to her daddy, her sister, the toys and dog, and the world around her."

"What does Mother Teresa mean to you?"

"Everybody knows her. She is a personality in the newspapers and on television; she won the Nobel Peace prize; they call her a living saint. But I was able to understand the real meaning of her life only when I visited Calcutta. Mother Teresa cannot be understood apart from Calcutta. It was only there that she was able to carry out her desire to work for the poor. This was for me the first discovery. The other discovery deeply affected me and even caused something of a personal crisis."

"What was the second discovery?"

"My contact with the children was a moving experience, but meeting the Missionaries of Charity was even more profound. Around this saint, Mother Teresa, there are also thousands of others who are saints. They are not known; no one speaks of them; but they accomplish incredible things.

"We have grown accustomed to a Christianity of excuses. Yes, Jesus said that it is necessary to give everything to the poor, but we are content to give of our superfluous goods. Mother Teresa takes that teaching seriously, and so do her Sisters. And if she can do it and the Missionaries of Charity can do it, then the teaching can be taken seriously.

"This discovery forced me to make an examination of conscience. I came to the realization that I could no longer hide behind good intentions. Live your life, occupied as it is with a thousand tasks, but keep before you the desire to put the Gospel teaching into practice. The charism of Mother Teresa works its way into you."

The word "charism" is derived from the Greek word *charis*, meaning grace. According to Catholic teaching, sanctifying grace is infused into the soul at baptism; charismatic graces, on the other hand, are described by St. Paul as special gifts given to chosen souls for the good of the faithful. In the vocabulary of Max Weber, a charism is a special quality in individuals who are called to exercise some special function of leadership; for example, extraordinary dedication to a noble cause, heroic strength or outstanding valor.

"In your opinion, Mrs. Forzini, what is Mother Teresa's charism?"

"I have heard her speak many times — at meetings, congresses and religious ceremonies. She doesn't say anything extraordinary; she says what we have always heard from our priests: love one another as brothers and sisters, trust in divine providence, have confidence. But she doesn't simply say those things; she practices them. They are extraordinary in the sense that she actually lives them. She lives them every day; they permeate her entire being."

A BAD HEART

On September 5, 1989, the first news flash was sent around the world: "Mother Teresa of Calcutta has had a heart attack. Her condition is critical." In the following days medical bulletins were released by the Woodlands Nursing Home in Calcutta, but the news was not good. Mother Teresa's condition was deteriorating. The doctors at the hospital consulted with Mother Teresa's cardiologist, Dr. Vincenzo Giulio Bilotta of Salvator Mundi Hospital in Rome. He is a specialist in cardiology, blood circulation, gerontology and geriatrics. He had studied under the famous American cardiologists, Dr. De Bakey and Dr. Cooley. Here is his diagnosis: "Mother Teresa did not suffer a heart attack but a coronary ischemia, which is something that precedes an authentic heart attack. She suffers from an irregular angina, caused by blocked arteries. The blood is not pumped through the heart as it should be. However, I do not believe that this coronary insufficiency is due to an excess of cholesterol because she eats very little and her food is almost devoid of fats. In this respect, her diet is exemplary. I think that her heart is worn out from the anxiety and preoccupation that she experiences for others.

"I saw her in Rome at the end of July and she was very tired. Once again I advised her not to wear herself out but to be a bit less active. But she had to leave for a long journey, with stops in Kenya, the United States, and Poland — her customary holy folly."

On the evening of September 5, Dr. Bilotta received a phone call from the superior of the Missionaries of Charity in Calcutta: "Doctor, come at once. Mother is ill." But Dr. Bilotta could not leave Rome; he was caring for some patients who were critically ill. Instead, a conference by radio was set up between Rome and Calcutta via New York. The doctors at Woodlands Nursing Home in Calcutta described the symptoms: high fever, vomiting, sharp chest pains, rapid heart beat, and blockage on the left side of the heart. Both the Indian doctors and the Italian cardiologist decided on an emergency procedure to clean out the artery.

Three days later the three superiors of the houses in Rome — Sister Agnel, Sister Martin and Sister Michael Joseph — went to Dr. Bilotta and insisted that he leave for Calcutta as soon as possible. It was September 9, a Saturday, and the Indian Embassy was closed. Dr. Bilotta did not have a visa for entering India, but in the name of Mother Teresa, they managed to cut through the Indian bureaucracy, which is one of the most intricate in the world. On Sunday morning the Embassy was opened at dawn and the consul issued a visa for Dr. Bilotta. At ten o'clock on the same morning he was at Fiumicino Airport to leave for New Delhi at eleven o'clock.

* * * * *

"When Mother Teresa saw me enter the room in the coronary unit of the hospital, she slumped down in her bed. She was under constant monitoring and was receiving oxygen. Her first words were an expression of concern that the doctors at the hospital might take offense at my arrival. 'These doctors,' she said, 'are caring for me with such competence and such love. I don't want them to feel annoyed because we sent for you. Please be tactful and don't embarrass your Indian colleagues.'

"Mother Teresa's condition was so serious that I feared she could be at the end of her life. The doctors had inserted a temporary pacemaker, fearing — and justifiably so — that the blockage might cause an occlusion which would result in cardiac arrest. Then there was the high fever that had to be diagnosed. I knew Mother Teresa's medical history and I knew that in the past she had contracted malaria. Hence, my diagnosis was that she had suffered an attack of malaria which in turn had affected the heart. The doctors had not administered any antibiotics for fear that she might be allergic to them. I assumed the responsibility of prescribing chloramphenicol, which is an antimalarial antibiotic. In the following days the fever subsided, the blockage was dissolved, and Mother Teresa was able to leave the hospital in order to convalesce in one of the houses of the Missionaries of Charity."

Dr. Bilotta returned to Rome on September 17, a Sunday, and scarcely had time to put down his suitcase when he received a phone call from Mother Teresa. She thanked him and then reminded him not to forget the task she had assigned to him.

"How could I possibly forget? One day, when she was still in very critical condition, I saw her trying to write a letter in spite of her pain. I forbade her to tire herself, so she put the paper and pen aside, but the next day she gave me the letter which she had finished secretly. 'I have disobeyed you, Doctor, but you will pardon me when I tell you to whom this letter is addressed. It is a letter to the Holy Father and I want you to deliver it to him in person.' She did not tell me what she had written.

"And how is Mother Teresa now?"

"The diagnosis is chronic coronary pathology that is getting worse. If she were younger, she could undergo surgery, but this operation can be performed safely only on patients under the age of 65. Anyone else in Mother Teresa's condition would be an invalid, but she has extraordinary energy and unusual spiritual power. What also helps her is a natural sense of humor that enables her to pay little or no attention to the trials of life. She once said to the Sisters: 'Doctor Bilotta says that I have a bad heart, but all of you know that I have a good heart, so there is nothing to fear.' She has also written: 'When suffering comes to us, we accept it with a smile. It is a great gift of God to be able to accept with a smile whatever he gives us and whatever he asks of us'."

* * * * *

"Dr. Bilotta, when did you first meet Mother Teresa?"

"Mother Teresa had her first heart problems in 1980. I took care of her, but she has also taken care of me."

At that time Mother Teresa was a patient in Salvator Mundi Hospital in Rome. She was confined to bed for two and a half months. She had neglected her health and suddenly began to have cardiac pains. Dr. Bilotta insisted that a long recovery was absolutely necessary, but she replied: "That is impossible. Tomorrow I must be in London to speak to 25,000 people who will assemble in Hyde Park." But later she realized that with her heart condition she should not go, so she obeyed the doctor. "If God wills this for me, it must mean that he has other plans for me."

During the critical period of her illness, Mother Teresa constantly repeated: "All for Jesus." She received visits from some very important people, including King Baldwin and Queen Fabiola, as well as a telephone call from Indira Gandhi in India. Mother Teresa commented: "Why do they bother so much about me?"

When she was dismissed from the hospital, Dr. Bilotta recommended that she live a more tranquil life, without preoccupation and with less travelling. Mother Teresa listened to him attentively, frequently nodding in agreement, but in the end she said: "Dear Doctor, if God wills that I die, he knows when and where it will happen." Now, whenever Dr. Bilotta sees her boarding a plane or speaking in a crowded stadium, he thinks that he has never had such a rebellious patient.

"I took care of her but she has also taken care of me. She has given me what a mother gives her child, not only in a spiritual sense, but also in a practical way. She has taught me how to face life and anxiety with serenity and common sense. My interior growth has been fostered by Mother Teresa. She has taken me by the hand, as my own mother did when I was a boy, and helped me to grow up.

"I come from a family in southern Italy. I was born in Lamezia Terme. My father died in 1946 as the result of a fall from a horse. I was sixteen years old at the time and my mother raised me and my seven sisters. She provided all of us with an education, at the cost of great sacrifice. She taught us to love one another and cultivated in us a spirit of giving.

"After I graduated, I became what is called a man of the world. I travelled much and had many experiences in foreign countries, especially in the United States. I was keen on becoming someone and being accepted socially, to enjoy all the benefits of success. Those desires became stronger in me than the sense of values inculcated in me by my mother. But when I met Mother Teresa, a sense of filial and maternal friendship was born between her and me. I have often seen in her the face of my own mother, the gentleness and the determination of my mother."

* * * * *

The first time that Dr. Bilotta visited Mother Teresa in 1980, he said to her: "I am a doctor for the Congregation for the Causes of Saints and I have written a great deal about saints. But I have never touched a saint with my own hands."

Mother Teresa laughed and said: "Dear Doctor, we are all saints if we do our work well. You too are a saint because you help those who are suffering."

"But unlike you, I get paid."

"And that is right. You have studied; you have a family; and you must maintain your professional standing. But you should never act as did an Indian doctor whom I met when he was leaving the home of a poor family as I was entering. There was no furniture in the house and I asked the head of the family what had happened to it. He replied: 'We had to sell it in order to pay the doctor's bill.'"

* * * * *

When she was released from the hospital after her first heart attack, Mother Teresa said to Dr. Bilotta: "You know the suffering of the sick, but you do not know the humiliation of the poor. Come with me; I'll take you to see my poor people. And I want you to know that this is a great privilege for you." They walked together to a house on Carlo Cattaneo Street near the *Stazione Termini*, the central railroad station in Rome. It is the house of the Missionaries of Charity who take care of the vagrants. Dr. Bilotta watched Mother Teresa bend over them with an expression of love. "I have observed at close range her dedication to the poor. I have thought that in each one of us there is a little of Mother Teresa. It is hidden in the depths of our being, but wants to express itself in goodness and in trustful self-giving.

"There is a trace of refinement in Mother Teresa that shows itself in little gestures. I once went with her to the house on Casilina Street, where the postulants live. Mother Teresa was lodged in a small hut at the rear of the kitchen garden; perhaps it was once a chicken-coop. To get to it, we had to walk on a path made of cement blocks, but it was so narrow that we would have had to walk in single file. She paid no attention to my protests but insisted that I should walk on the smooth path while she walked beside me on the muddy, uneven ground. She always acts in this courteous manner, but especially when she is dealing with the poorest of her poor people. Then it is as if she is the lowliest creature on earth kneeling before the Lord of all the world.

"One day Mother Teresa suggested that I dedicate my

family to the Sacred Heart of Jesus. We all agreed joyfully — my wife, our two daughters and myself. We did it on July 10, 1985, on a very hot afternoon in the scorching heat of the Roman summer. Besides Mother Teresa, Father O'Keefe, a Jesuit who had celebrated our matrimony, was also present. My wife had prepared some iced tea, and after the ceremony she offered some to our guests. Mother Teresa refused it with a smile, saying: 'Thank you, but according to our rule, we do not accept anything in the homes we visit. Usually they are the homes of the poor, and the poor are willing to take the food out of their own mouths to give it to us.'

"The humorous part of this incident was the expression on the faces of Father O'Keefe and my family. We were all feeling the heat and wanted a cool drink, but after Mother Teresa declined, no one else dared to pick up the glass of iced tea."

* * * * *

From her bed in the hospital in Calcutta, Mother Teresa wrote a letter for the Eucharistic Congress that was being held in Seoul, Korea, in October, 1989. This is an excerpt:

Conversion is love in action between God and the soul. The principal obstacle to conversion is sin. That is why the tenderness of God's love is so great that he gave us Jesus to wash away all our sins. He does this in confession through the merits of his Precious Blood. For that reason we go to confession and we become sinners without sin. This is true conversion: the love of God in the vivifying action of tender and merciful love. The pure of heart can see God in every person. Then naturally such a person will want to share the joy of love with one's own family and neighbors, especially those who have done us harm or those whom we have harmed. This is truly the fruit of authentic conversion because where there is love, there is God.

In that letter Mother Teresa suggests that people say the prayer "The Radiant Christ," composed by Cardinal Newman. She transcribed it in its entirety, inviting us to "make this prayer our own, because we also desire the fullness of conversion which is total abandonment to Christ." This is the prayer:

Dear Jesus, help me to spread your fragrance everywhere I go. Flood my soul with your spirit and life. Penetrate and possess my whole being so utterly that my life may be only a radiance of yours.

Shine through me and be so in me that every soul I come in contact with may feel your presence in my soul. Let them look up, and see no longer me, but only Jesus!

Stay with me and then I shall begin to shine as you shine, so to shine as to be a light to others. The light, O Jesus, will be all from you, shining on others through me. Let me thus praise you in the way which you love best, by shining on those around me.

Let me preach you without preaching, not by my words, but by my example, by the catching force, the sympathetic influence of what I do, the evident fullness of the love my heart bears to you. Amen.

GRAVEN ON
THE PALMS OF MY HANDS

T he only close living relative of Mother Teresa is a niece, the daughter of her brother Lazar, who died in 1981. Her name is Age, after Mother Teresa's blood sister. She lives in Palermo and is married to Joseph Guttadauro Mancinelli, who runs a clothing store. They have two children, Dominic, age 24, and Maximilian, age 22.

Age is a beautiful brunette and very elegant. She resembles Mother Teresa as a young girl in the photo we described previously, and especially in her glance. In the parlor of her home she has a large collection of ceramic containers for spices. They are called *albarelli*, and at one time they were used by chemists and pharmacists. Boccaccio referred to *albarelli d'unguenti colmi*. The collection is not foreign to the profession of Mother Teresa's father because among his many business enterprises he also had a pharmacy. Lazar, Age's father, was a salesman of medicines and he brought the *albarelli* to Italy. The window of Age's home looks out on Porta Felice, and down below, one can see the marina sparkling in the sun. Curiously enough, there is not a single photo of Mother Teresa either on the walls or on the writing desk that contains photos of the children — two very blond boys. "I have the photo of my aunt in the bedroom, where I can look at it when I wake up in the morning," says Age, smiling. She hastens to get the latest photos that Mother Teresa had sent her. In all the pictures Mother Teresa is holding a child — an Indian child, a black child or a white child. On the margin of each photo Mother Teresa has written a quotation from the prophet Isaiah: "I will not forget you. Behold, I have graven you on the palms of my hands. I have called you by name. You are mine. You are precious in my eyes. I love you." Each photo is dedicated to a member of the family: "Dear Age. Dear Peppe. Dear Dominic. Dear Maximilian." Then she added, in her large clear script: "God bless you."

Mother Teresa had used the words of the prophet Isaiah to express her affection for her niece and family. Those words are very dear to her and she has repeated them many times. "I am convinced," she said, "that each time we say 'Our Father,' God looks at the palms of his hands. *I have graven you on the palms of my hands....* God looks at the palms of his hands and sees us there."

* * * * *

In a photo of Age's father, Lazar Bojaxhiu, taken when he was a young man, he has blue eyes, a straightforward glance and the imposing physique of an artillery officer. His resemblance to Mother Teresa was much greater in later years, when he was ill and his face was much thinner, thus making his eyes and his large nose more prominent.

Age says: "Our family is Albanian, and we are very Albanian. We are not a numerous people — three million in Albania, three million in Kosovo, which declared its independence from Yugoslavia, and the rest dispersed throughout the world. But we are united by our strong sense of nationality. The most famous Albanian is Mother Teresa, and that is paradoxical for a nation whose government once imposed atheism by an article in its Constitution.

"I have to laugh when I read in some newspapers that Mother Teresa was born into a family of peasants. The Bojaxhiu family were landowners and professional people, at least as long as my grandfather Kole was alive. He had a pharmacy degree and owned forests and saw mills. His wife, Drane, my grandmother, must have been a very intelligent woman with modern ideas. She wanted all three of her children to study and she provided the same education for her two daughters as she had for her son, something unusual in those days. Perhaps she foresaw that her children would travel around the world. She remained alone at home after her husband died. Lazar was studying in France, Age was in Vienna, and Agnes was in the convent in Ireland. My grandmother used to speak with pride about her children, who were getting their education outside the narrow confines of Albania.

* * * * *

Mother Teresa was always reluctant to speak about herself, and when she spoke of her family, she always did so with succinct statements. "We were a happy family. We were always very close to one another, especially after the death of my father. We lived, one for the other."

The parents of Mother Teresa were Kole (Nicholas) Bojaxhiu and Drane Bernai. They had three children: Lazar, born in 1907, Agnes, born in 1910, and Age, born in 1913. Kole Bojaxhiu came from a family of Albanian tradesmen, and he himself was a well-to-do business man. He settled in Skopje, where his first enterprise was to open a pharmacy. He later extended his interests to other commercial ventures, ranging from real estate to grocery stores to timber. He was much inclined to music, as is Mother Teresa, who has a good singing voice and as a girl played the mandolin very well. In a photo taken in 1912, Kole appears as a trumpet player in the municipal band of Skopje. He was also interested in politics and attended the meetings of patriots who promoted Albanian causes. When Albania obtained its independence on November 28, 1912, there was a great celebration in the Bojaxhiu household. Curri, Hasan Prishtina and Sabri Qytezi, who had been active in the movement against the Turks, were also present. Lazar, who was five years old at the time, remembered the songs of victory, the toasts, and even the little fire that was built in the middle of the room to celebrate their freedom from the yoke of the Ottoman Empire, which had lasted 450 years. [The following year, however, the great European powers dismembered Albania, leaving half of its territory and population beyond the frontier.]

Kole Bojaxhiu died suddenly in 1919. As a member of the community council, he had gone to Belgrade with his colleagues, and while there he suffered an attack, perhaps of peritonitis. The Italian consul took him home in his carriage, but Kole died after emergency treatment proved futile. Practically the entire city attended the funeral, since he had been a very prominent citizen.

With the death of Kole, the task of raising three little children fell squarely on the shoulders of Drane, who courageously faced the economic hardship caused by the death of her husband. She opened a sewing and embroidery shop in her home, specializing in wedding gowns and elegant dresses for social affairs.

Drane was a woman of great faith, as Mother Teresa recalls: "My mother was a saintly woman. She trained us in the love of God and of neighbor. She taught us to love God above all things."

Drane was also very strict in the formation of her children, as Lazar later recalled: "Mama required us to ask permission for everything. Most of the time she granted it, but at the same time she insisted that we should conduct ourselves so well, both at home and in school, that we would be an example to our companions. She said that we should do good without making a show of it, with the same naturalness that one would throw a stone in the sea. She had the same passion for religion that my father had for politics. We called her 'Mama Loke'; not only we, but our relatives and neighbors...." The word *loke* is difficult to translate into English. It signifies affection accompanied by respect. In 1974, a few days before her death, Drane sent a photo to her daughter, Mother Teresa, whom she had not seen in 45 years. On it she wrote: "Gonxha, I kiss you. Mama Loke." Both as a child and as an adolescent, Agnes was studious and joyful; she had a passion for poetry and song. When the Albanian language was banished from the schools in Skopje, which had become a Yugoslav city, Agnes followed the courses in Serbian Croatian without any difficulty. She was always gifted in languages. In high school the idea of becoming a missionary was still a long way off. During those years her interests were teaching, writing poetry and composing music. She did eventually become a teacher and as a novice she was still writing poetry. One of her poems, composed on December 9, 1928, on board the ship to India, begins as follows:

> I leave the house that gives light to my heart,
> My country, my entire family.
> My goal is Bengal, prostrate with suffering,
> A land dear to me, although it is a foreign land.

Personal choices and historical changes brought about the separation of the Bojaxhiu family. In 1934 Drane and Age moved to Tirana, where Age worked as a radio announcer and Lazar was an officer in the army of King Zog. Drane's only comfort was her daughter Age, who had not married so that she could remain with her mother. Drane died there, regretting that she had not been able to see her daughter Agnes, who was a missionary in India. In the meantime, Lazar had emigrated to Italy.

* * * * *

"Mrs. Guttadauro, why did your father Lazar decide to settle in Italy?"

"He was an officer in the Albanian army when Italy invaded Albania in 1939. Like many others, he was assigned to serve in the Italian army. During the entire war he was stationed in Turin, Italy, as a career officer in the artillery. At the end of the war he resigned as a colonel. He never wanted to renounce his Albanian citizenship in order to become an Italian citizen. This was also a factor in his resignation from the Italian army.

"He met my mother, Maria Sanguigni, in Lucca. I am their only daughter. My father could not return to Albania because after the war the Communist regime of Enver Hoxha was in power. A friend advised my parents to move to Sicily and start a business in wholesale medicine. My father worked at this business for the rest of his life. He died of cancer in 1981 at the age of 73."

"What did he tell you about the time when he and his sisters were young?"

"My father's recollections were always about the three of them together. My grandmother assigned chores to each of the three children, but my father was a bit unruly. His sisters did their chores and then finished the ones that had been assigned to him. For example, in the evening each one had to take turns polishing everybody's shoes. All three of them were lively, but my father was more capricious. Sometimes his mother would punish him by sending him to bed without any supper, but his sisters would always carry food to him secretly.

"My father and Mother Teresa finally had a visit after 40 years and they recalled many incidents of their childhood, laughing at many of them. I don't know which ones they talked about because they were speaking Albanian."

* * * * *

Agnes was 18 years old when she went to Ireland to join the Sisters of Loreto. Before leaving, she wrote to her brother Lazar, who had just graduated from the military academy as a second-lieutenant. He was living far away from home and he did not realize that his little sister's plans had reached that point. He immediately sent her an indignant letter: how could she sacrifice her life by burying herself in some remote convent?

Agnes' reply was a bit sharp: "You think that you are very important because you are an officer in the service of the king of a few million subjects. I am entering the service of the King of the entire world. According to you, which of us has chosen the better post?"

Thereafter Lazar would speak with pride of his sister, who had chosen the better post: "Agnes is an officer like I am. She could have gone to military school. She has an incredible strength of will, like our mother. She is disciplined; she follows precise regulations; and she has outstanding gifts for command. She is a real leader."

Mother Teresa's first visit with Lazar after the 40-year interval took place during her first visit to Rome in November, 1960. Lazar had come up from Palermo with his wife Maria and their daughter Age. This is how Age describes that visit:

"Papa and my aunt talked rapidly together in Albanian. My aunt was already famous, but Papa still treated her like his little sister. He told me that he had remembered her as being taller, even taller than me. Papa was not a really tall man, but he had to bend down low to embrace her. He was greatly moved to see how small and frail she had become. It was the result of her hard work; she had always led a life of intense activity and privation."

"Did you ever go to visit the Bojaxhiu family home in Skopje?"

"No, everything was destroyed by the earthquake in 1963. Mother Teresa has visited the places of her childhood but she told me that nothing remains of the house, the church or the school. Even our chapel in the cemetery no longer exists. Everything was destroyed."

The earthquake that demolished Skopje occurred on July

26, 1963. The results were: 1,070 dead, 3,300 injured, and 140,000 left homeless. Mother Teresa returned to her home town to open a house on June 8, 1978. She took four Sisters with her to work in Skopje and she said to the mayor: "You have given one person, and I have returned four."

"And when did you see your aunt again after that first visit in Rome?"

"Every time she came to Rome we left Palermo to visit her. In December of 1979 she was awarded the Nobel Peace Prize and Papa and I went to Oslo, Norway. We met her on the evening of her arrival, at St. Joseph Institute, where she was staying. Papa said to me: 'She is always smaller, but she is always better.'

"Mother Teresa was very happy to receive the Nobel Peace Prize. In her acceptance speech, in front of all those important people, she did not want to miss the opportunity to speak against abortion in a Protestant country that had legalized it some time before. I still remember the headlines in the newspapers."

* * * * *

Mother Teresa learned about being awarded the Nobel Peace Prize in a telephone call from the Prime Minister of India. She said: "It is for God's glory," and then continued to work on the accounts with Sister Camillus. In the hours following, she was amazed at all the telegrams that were arriving, and she was especially delighted to read those from Tito, the President of Yugoslavia, and from the Communist government of China.

She arrived in Oslo on December 9 for the conferral of the prize. An arctic wind was blowing and at the airport the lady from the Indian Embassy, shocked at seeing Mother Teresa clad only in a cotton sari and the customary gray sweater, placed a cape around her shoulders.

The following day, December 10, 1979, Mother Teresa spoke in the auditorium of the university. In front of her were seated King Olaf V, the academic community, and leaders of the scientific and political world, all dressed in formal attire, both men and women. Her sari was a symbol of the challenge of humility in the face of power, and she took advantage of it. As she always did before speaking in public, she traced the sign of the cross on her lips with her thumb and then she invited the audience to recite with her the prayer of St. Francis of Assisi: "Lord, make me an instrument of thy peace." She had arranged to have mimeographed copies of the text distributed to the assembly. [Later she told the Sisters: "They all said the prayer and, as you know, there are not many Catholics in Norway."]

After the prayer, she delivered her discourse, speaking extemporaneously as usual. She was very firm in her defense of life. "The greatest destroyer of peace is abortion. And we who are standing here — our parents wanted us. We would not be here if our parents had wanted to do that to us. Our children, we want them, we love them. But what of the millions who are dying by the deliberate will of the mother. And that is what is the greatest destroyer of peace today. Because if a mother can kill her own child, what is left but for me to kill you and you to kill me; there is nothing in between. And this I appeal in India. I appeal everywhere. Let us bring back the child, this year being the year of the child! What have we done for the child?" Then Mother Teresa turned to King Olaf and cried out: "I repeat, Your Majesty, abortion is murder!"

On the plane during the return trip to Rome, the stewardess distributed the newspapers. Large headlines reported the turmoil caused by Mother Teresa's words in a country where abortion is peacefully practiced. As soon as she arrived in Rome, she became sick with the flu. In spite of a fever, she went to see the Holy Father, and she was entrusted with a charge much more prestigious than the Nobel Peace Prize. Pope John Paul II urged her: "Go and speak that way all over."

* * * * *

"We had only a short visit in Oslo," Age continued, "because my aunt was busy with many visits and interviews. On the other hand, in September of 1989, when she was recovering in the hospital in Calcutta after her heart attack, we were with her for 12 days. It all depended on her. We were not sure that she would recover. She thought it was foolish for the doctors to take such special care of her. She was seriously ill and she went through a very difficult time. Nevertheless, whenever she had any periods of relief, she would write letters, propped up with pillows. I begged her not to wear herself out, but she answered: 'That would not be right. So many friends have sent me good wishes; they deserve to receive an answer.'

"As soon as she felt somewhat better, she began to call in the Sister superiors in order to organize new projects. She is a good manager who makes important decisions from one moment to the next. She may be ready to fly to America, but suddenly she decides: 'I will go to America later; first I must go to another place.' But her activity is always the result of her spirituality and her prayer.

"During those 12 days visiting her in the hospital in Calcutta, I had some tense moments at her side. We had never before had the opportunity to be so close together. Thank God, I understand English very well, so we had no difficulty in conversing with each other. We spoke for long periods of time and I learned many things.

"When my father was dying in the hospital in Rome in 1981, Mother Teresa came to see him every day. I believe that those daily visits helped my father to accept his death."

There is a letter written by Mother Teresa after the death of her brother, and it reads: "All her life our mother dreamed that Lazar would eventually return home. He was the only son, and she loved him more than her own life. At last he is with her. Lazar had a beautiful death and he has returned home to God."

Age said: "I keep many of Mother Teresa's letters, brief messages that she has sent me through the years. In our family we are not given to writing long letters. Instead, we call each other by phone, and my aunt always reminds me to stay close to my mother, who is 80 years old.

"We all call Mother Teresa a saint, but we all consider her to be very normal, witty and ready for a joke. She has an innate gift for improving the people that she meets. When we are with her we experience an impulse to do good and to be helpful to others. Later it passes, at least in the sense that one does not experience a special inspiration, but what remains is a feeling of peace in oneself and with others.

"Mother Teresa once told me when I was with her in India: 'I would like one of your sons to become a priest.' But you know, my husband is a business man and the boys are inclined to financial affairs. Maximilian is studying at Bocconi University in Milan and Dominic is studying commerce and finance here in Palermo. It is unlikely that either of them will become a priest, but my aunt continues to hope for it. 'God's ways are infinite,' she kept repeating during those days in the hospital."

LOWLY SERVANT

U nder the vaulted ceiling of the church the choir intones the opening hymn for the ceremony that is to follow:

> My soul proclaims the greatness of the Lord.
> My spirit rejoices in God my Savior,
> For he has looked with favor on his lowly servant.

It is November 27, 1990, a cold and clear Friday under the Roman sun. In the Basilica of Sts. John and Paul on the Coelian Hill, ten novices will make their religious profession. Their parents, relatives and friends are seated in the front pews.

In the center of the nave of the basilica there is a little table on which there are ears of grain, a basket of fruit and a ciborium containing hosts. At the main altar a bishop is celebrating the Mass, accompanied by some 20 concelebrants. The flowers around the altar are those used for a wedding ceremony in Italy — bouquets of gladioli, white carnations and bridal wreath. The TV and newspaper cameras are all focused on Mother Teresa and her group of novices. Mother follows the liturgy, sometimes standing, sometimes kneeling and touching the floor with her forehead, as is her custom. In spite of her arthritis, she is still able to do that.

Mother Teresa is totally absorbed in prayer, yet nothing

escapes her notice. Like a master of ceremonies, she directs the movements of the novices with a glance of her eyes or a slight gesture. Now they group together, now they form a circle, now they stand single file and advance one by one. Each novice receives two saris, two tunics made of the cloth that is used for bags of rice or flour, a pair of sandals, a shopping bag of coarse cloth with wooden handles, a metal spoon and plate, a rosary and a crucifix. Later she will send them into the world, two by two.

> *Then he summoned the twelve and began to send them out in pairs, giving them authority over the unclean spirits. And he instructed them to take nothing for the journey except a staff — no bread, no haversack no coppers for their purses. They were to wear sandals but he added: 'Do not take a spare tunic.' ... So they set off to preach repentance; and they cast out many devils, and anointed many sick people with oil and cured them* (Mk 6:7-13).

* * * * *

When she founded the Missionaries of Charity, Mother Teresa stipulated four requisites for becoming a member of the Congregation: "Any young woman who wants to enter our Congregation must be healthy in mind and body, must be able to learn, must be gifted with a great deal of common sense, and must be motivated by a right intention. If she meets these four requirements, she may be invited to come and observe our work. She will enter one of our houses and come into close contact with the poor, the people and the Sisters. She will work with them, pray with them, live with them. In the end she will decide if this is the way that God wants her to follow."

The minimum age for entrance is sixteen. What in other religious institutes is called the period of postulancy, Mother Teresa calls "Come and See," the words of Jesus to his disciples.

This period lasts for six months and is followed by another six months of postulancy and then two years of novitiate formation. The Missionaries of Charity spend six years in temporary vows. Then, before making their final profession of perpetual vows, they return to the novitiate for a year of more intense spiritual life.

But the period of testing is not yet finished. Before being admitted to final and definitive profession, the Sister returns to her family for fifteen days. There, in the midst of her loved ones in the environment in which she was born and grew up, the Sister has the last chance to turn back or to embrace forever the difficult but happy life offered by Mother Teresa and the Missionaries of Charity.

The Sisters live according to a rule, and their lifestyle is the same in all the houses throughout the world — in the slums of Calcutta, in the ghetto of the scavengers in Cairo, in the various sections of Rome, in the *favelas* of Rio de Janeiro, in the various houses in the United States.

The Sisters rise at 4:30 in the morning. Kissing the sari, they say this prayer: "This habit reminds me that I do not belong to the world and its vanities. The world means nothing to me, and I mean nothing to the world. May this habit be for me like a baptismal dress and help me keep my heart free from sin."

The Sisters then put their sandals on their bare feet as they pray: "With spontaneous and free will, O Jesus, I shall follow wherever you go, in search of souls, without any recompense and solely for love of you."

Then the Sisters go to the chapel, genuflect before the crucifix, and spend a half hour in mental prayer. This is followed by the Eucharistic liturgy, which is the spiritual fulcrum of their life of dedication and the starting point for their daily tasks. They receive Communion, which is their first daily encounter with Christ, whom they will see in the following hours incarnate in the lepers, the abandoned children, the aged or in those suffering from AIDS.

As soon as they leave the chapel, they wash in a bucket of soapy water the sari that they had worn the previous day, and then hang it in the sun to dry. In India, their breakfast consists of tea and *chapati*, a flat cake made out of flour. In other parts of the world it may be tea and bread. At about 8:00 o'clock they leave the house with a companion for their work among the poor, reciting the rosary as they go, either walking or on the bus or street car.

The Sisters return home for lunch, which consists of rice or soup and some vegetables, eaten from their aluminum plate. This is followed by a half hour of rest, which is needed after having been active for more than eight hours and in view of the hours of work that await them in the afternoon. They are back on the street by 2:00 o'clock in the afternoon. When they return home in the late afternoon, they have an hour of adoration in the chapel before supper, and after supper they have a half hour of recreation. Mother Teresa is insistent on community prayer and community recreation.

Before retiring for the night, which is usually around 10:00 o'clock, the Missionaries of Charity ask themselves four questions, which are an examination of conscience that leads to prayer of petition: "Do I know that my wealth consists in possessing the Kingdom and my happiness consists in being poor? Am I totally at the service of Christ? Is my obedience truly active and responsible, and is it an expression of my love for the Lord? Have I been able to see the abandoned Christ in the poor whom I have met today?" Each Sister then asks the Lord to enable her to answer each question in the affirmative, every evening for the rest of her life.

* * * * *

Let us return to the ceremony in the Basilica of Sts. John and Paul. After the liturgy of the word and the ritual chant, there is a period of silence. Then the director of the novices calls each one by name and each one responds in a loud voice: "O Lord, you have called me. Here I am." This is followed by each novice reciting the formula of religious profession: "I promise chastity, poverty, obedience and free service to the poorest of the poor, according to the Constitutions of the Missionaries of Charity, for one year and eleven days."

After each Sister has made her profession, a procession is formed and goes to the little table in the middle of the basilica to carry the gifts to the main altar. The newly professed carry the ciborium with the hosts, the parents bring the baskets containing bread, fruit, ears of grain or Indian incense. Mother Teresa, at the end of the line, carries the most significant gift: a parchment containing the list of names of the newly professed Missionaries of Charity. When the little procession disperses after placing the gifts on the altar, Mother Teresa gives a brief talk that she has repeated hundreds of times, but it always seems new:

"Jesus has come to give you the good news. The good news is that God loves us and wants us to love one another.

To make it easy for us to love one another, Jesus has said: Whatever you do to the least of my brethren, you have done unto me. If you give a glass of water to the thirsty, you give it to me; if you embrace the abandoned baby, you embrace me; if you give food to the hungry, you give it to me. I was hungry, I was naked, I was homeless, and you have fed me, you have clothed me, you have given me shelter.

A pure heart can see God, and if we see God, we can love one another as God loves us.

The fruit of prayer is faith. The fruit of faith is love. The fruit of love is service. The fruit of service is peace."

* * * * *

On many occasions Mother Teresa has described the Missionaries of Charity this way: "Above all, we are religious. We are not social workers, teachers, nurses or doctors. We are

159

religious. We serve Jesus in the poor. We visit him, care for him, clothe him in the poor, the abandoned, the sick, the orphans, the dying.

"All that we do — our prayer, our work, our suffering — is for Jesus. We do something beautiful for Jesus. Our life has no reason, no motive, no meaning apart from him. This is something that many do not understand."

Then there are the three regulations that she has given the Sisters regarding their deportment on the street and in their work: poverty, silence and a smile.

Poverty: "More than any other religious order, we need poverty, true poverty. Poverty gives us the detachment and freedom that are necessary if we are to understand the very poorest with whom we work."

Silence: "We need silence in order to be able to touch souls. What is important is not what we say, but what God says to us and through us."

A Smile: "I don't want you to work miracles with rudeness. I prefer that you make mistakes with gentleness. Smile, always smile."

THE INTERVIEW

I went to see Mother Teresa at Number 222 Via Casilina, one of the six houses of the Missionaries of Charity in Rome. I had in my purse a list of a hundred questions that I would never be able to ask, because first of all we say the rosary and then at the end there is never enough time. I once had another list of questions ready when I went with a group of journalists for an interview with Mother Teresa. She ended the interview after a few words and then invited the journalists to pray with her. It was an exhilarating experience to see those werewolves of the press murmuring the forgotten Hail Mary.

One day I made an appointment to be at San Gregorio al Celio, the headquarters of the Missionaries of Charity in Rome. I could not believe that I had obtained an interview just for me. But Mother had been called away suddenly and in her place I found a glass of water and a card containing three words: "God bless you." I have had interviews that were professionally very fruitful and from which I emerged greatly edified but also frustrated because of their brevity. Mother Teresa is the despair of interviewers and biographers.

"I would rather wash a leper than answer the questions of journalists," she said with a flash of mock anger in her eyes. But since she is the most congenial person in the world, she always adds: "Your work is to interview and I must cooperate." Sometimes when she sees me approaching her with my tape recorder and pad, she exclaims: "Here again?" Then she will say to a Sister or some other person present: "This lady writes; she writes everything." But Mother Teresa doesn't say this with irritation but with patience and good humor.

Once in an airport, while she tried to extricate herself from a crowd of journalists who were shoving their microphones into her face and cameramen who were focusing their cameras on her, someone asked her what was her greatest suffering. She responded: "This."

When the news broke on October 10, 1979, that she had been awarded the Nobel Peace Prize, the customary battery of reporters laid siege to the entrance of the Motherhouse on Lower Circle Road. The next day, speaking to the Calcutta correspondent for the Associated Press, Mother Teresa made this comment: "Last evening it seemed as if all the vultures of Calcutta had a meeting here." Then she immediately softened the undiplomatic remark: "But even vultures can be beautiful."

Before the Nobel Peace Prize was awarded to her in Oslo, some journalists insisted on knowing something about Mother Teresa's life and background. She has never wanted to talk or write about herself and therefore she responded by giving the most succinct autobiography imaginable: "By blood and origin I am Albanian. I have Indian citizenship. I am a Catholic nun. By vocation I belong to the whole world. In my heart I belong entirely to the heart of Jesus."

Sometimes she answers interviewers with a touch of sarcasm, especially when their questions are critical of her work. For example, she has been asked why she doesn't teach the poor how to fish instead of giving them the fish free. She answered: "Our people are hardly able to stand on their feet. They are hungry or sick or disabled. They are not even able to handle a fishing pole. What I do is give them fish to eat until they are stronger. Then I will turn them over to you, and you can give them a fishing pole and teach them how to catch fish."

During a visit to Germany, when she was bothered by the

flash bulbs of the photographers, she turned to her German collaborator, Josepha Gosselke, and said: "I have made a contract with Jesus. For every photo they take of me, a soul will be released from purgatory. By now, purgatory should be empty."

Mother Teresa yields to the demands of the press at a personal sacrifice, but she recognizes its usefulness. "I am forced to suffer being a celebrity. I do it for the love of Jesus. When the newspapers and television speak of me, they speak of the poor, and in that way they focus attention on the poor. It's worthwhile to bear the burden."

In her speech on receiving the Nobel Peace Prize, she said: "If I don't go to heaven for some other reason, I'll go for all the publicity that surrounds me, because this has cleansed and purified me and made me ready for heaven."

* * * * *

I met Mother Teresa for the first time on March 1, 1979, in Rome. It was at the beautiful villa of the Accademia dei Lincei, where she had just received the Balzan Prize "for humaneness, peace and brotherhood among peoples." She greeted the authorities present, holding the parchment tied with blue ribbon and the check for 250 million lire. She seemed so very small. Her friend Indira Gandhi used to say of her: "She is very small, but there is nothing small about her."

Among the dignitaries who approached Mother Teresa to shake her hand and congratulate her were the President of Italy, Sandro Pertini, Giulio Andreotti, the professors of the Accademia, four State Ministers and a half dozen ambassadors. In a gesture that is typical of her, she cocked her head to one side and looked up at them. Over her sari she wore a lightweight gray sweater with a safety pin in place of a missing button. In spite of the cold of winter's end, she wore sandals on her bare feet. In her face, lined with hundreds of wrinkles, her eyes were shining with happiness.

With that same happy look on her face, Mother Teresa faced a group of journalists after the ceremony. Then began an unusual news conference in two different languages — the questions were from this world but the answers were from another. Without paying any attention to the first question that was asked, Mother Teresa began to talk about unwanted babies, abandoned babies and babies dying of hunger.

"Mother Teresa, instead of letting them live like that, wouldn't it be better if they had never been born?"

"Babies are the most beautiful gift of God. Every infant has a right to come into this world, wanted or not. Abortion is a crime committed in the womb of the mother."

"But Mother Teresa, isn't the quality of life more important than birth?"

"The first right is to be born. All others come afterwards."

"Mother Teresa, what sense does it make to live on a subhuman standard?"

"No one can judge the life of another. One homeless poor person told me: 'I have lived like an animal, but thanks to you, I die like an angel.' This is what has meaning."

"Mother Teresa, what do you think about launching a campaign against armaments?"

"I don't launch campaigns; I don't get involved in petitions or fund-raising; nor do I permit others to do it in my name. I am very strict about this. I can only suggest to governments: 'Give me the money you spend on arms. I know how to use it well'."

"Mother Teresa, don't you think that the Church spends too much time on superfluous activities instead of helping the poor?"

"We are the Church. We should not judge others, but ourselves. We shall be judged for what we have done to Jesus suffering, to Jesus abandoned, to Jesus hungry."

"Mother Teresa, isn't it almost impossible to live as a Christian in today's world?"

"Yes! In fact, it is *so* difficult that we cannot do it without the aid of prayer. We Catholics have the Body of Christ. This gives us strength. Jesus comes to us in the form of bread to show his love for us, in the form of a hungry person so we can feed him, naked so we can clothe him, homeless so we can give him shelter."

"Mother Teresa, are there still vocations to your order?"

"There is a constant increase. Young women come to me and say: 'I want a life of poverty, of love, of sacrifice.' I answer: 'Good, my daughter; those are the only things I can give you'."

"Mother Teresa, what do your Missionaries of Charity do in Rome?"

"Do you think that India is only in India? Then some night follow my Sisters to the Termini railroad station. You will see them picking up abandoned persons from the floor, the same as in Calcutta. But it gets colder in Rome and that is why fewer of them are seen in the streets."

"Mother Teresa, is your hair short or long?"

"It's shaved. I don't have time to do my hair."

"Mother Teresa, how can you preach the Gospel to someone whose stomach is empty?"

"There are various ways of doing it. It can be done this way...." (Mother Teresa stands up, extends her hands, and draws them back quickly. It is the gesture of a person who gives charity in a hasty, impersonal way.) "Or this way...." (She holds her hands together like a cup and extends them with compassion and tenderness. It is the gesture of a person who gives charity with compassion and love.) "There is a hunger for bread and a hunger for love. Some are naked because of a lack of clothing and some are naked because of a lack of human dignity. Jesus said: 'I was hungry and you gave me to eat. I was sick and you visited me. I was abandoned and you consoled me'."

* * * * *

At last I had been granted an interview just for me; Mother Teresa and I, alone in the silence of San Gregorio al Celio. This house of the Missionaries of Charity was formerly the chicken house of the Camaldolese monks. There are 35 Sisters there and the small cells open out on a corridor without a roof, but covered with a trellis. One can still see the drain in the cement pavement from the days when the building housed the chickens raised by the monks.

I had arranged the interview with the help of Sister Agnel, the superior of the Missionaries of Charity in Italy. She has been with Mother Teresa since 1969. When she joined the Missionaries of Charity, she had wanted to take as her religious name the baptismal name of mother Teresa, Agnes. But that name had already been taken by the first Sister who had joined the Congregation, so Mother Teresa said: "We shall change the name a little," and that is how Sister Agnel got her name.

It was the evening of April 26, 1990, that I arrived for this special interview. I had come to the appointment fearful that once again the interview would be cancelled because of some emergency or because Mother Teresa had suddenly made a change and was about to leave the house. But Mother Teresa was there, and she was waiting for me. She seemed to be smaller and more exhausted than the last time I had seen her. No doubt this was due to the heart attack that had necessitated a stay in the hospital in Calcutta and a long period of convalescence.

But Mother was there, in the former chicken house of the Camaldolese monks of San Gregorio, and she was waiting for me. Once again I felt the aura of her presence. I experienced the blessing that emanates from a person totally committed to God; it is a spiritual impact that the Indians call *darshan*, the awareness that one is in the presence of a superior being. The Hindu scriptures say that one moment in the presence of a saint cancels a mountain of sins. Therefore, people would rush to the place where Mahatma Gandhi was expected to pass so that they could experience the *darshan*. The same thing happens today when they see *Ma Teresa* in the streets of Calcutta.

* * * * *

"How are you, Mother Teresa?"

"I feel strong. I have come to Europe for three reasons: to open a house in Romania, to visit Albania, and to go to Czecho-slovakia."

Speaking in her customary laconic fashion, Mother Teresa gets to the point immediately, in accordance with the advice in Ecclesiastes: "Let your words be few."

I have in my purse the clippings from last week's newspapers. According to the *Corriere della Sera*, 'Teresa of Calcutta resigns.' *La Stampa* says: 'Teresa of Calcutta says good-bye to her mission.' In *La Reppublica* the headline reads: 'The humble resignation of Mother Teresa.' The article states that Mother Teresa has offered her resignation to Pope John Paul II as superior general of the Missionaries of Charity. The Pope has accepted it and a new superior general will be elected on September 8, at the General Chapter of the Congregation.

"So now you are retired, Mother Teresa?"

"No, I have not retired. The poor do not retire. I have simply resigned as superior general." She pauses for a moment and reaches across the table to take my hands. "I did not offer the resignation of Mother Teresa."

Then she explains: "We have a General Chapter in September and then someone else will take my place as superior general. I can give a hand to the Sisters while I am still here, to help them know what must be done, because many things are not understood until they are done. We shall elect a new superior general and I shall help her to know what she should do. But I shall be a Sister like the rest."

(Things, however, turned out differently at the General

Chapter. Mother Teresa was re-elected superior general of the Missionaries of Charity. That had happened every six years since 1960, when the first elections were held at a General Chapter. This time there were 103 voting members at the Chapter, and when the votes were counted, Mother Teresa received 102 votes.)

* * * * *

On August 27, 1990, Mother Teresa completed her eightieth year. She appeared to be more doubled over than ever, as if to shield and protect her weakened heart. But her spirit impelled her forward to Romania, Albania and Czechoslovakia. At Bucharest in Romania this "specialist" in healing the wounds of the world is awaited so that she can care for the victims of the latest plague. It is not the centuries-old malady of leprosy, although it attacks with the same destructive force, provokes the same fear and results in the same strict taboo. It is the plague of AIDS.

When the government fell in Romania, a scandal was revealed that had previously been hidden under the lid of the Communist kettle. Hundreds of babies in Bucharest were infected with AIDS. They had contracted the disease from transfusions of blood imported from Africa and administered without the slightest degree of control or caution. The babies were consigned to a filthy section of the hospitals and were in a state of extreme neglect because the nurses refused to touch them for fear of contagion. While the world shuddered in horror, Mother Teresa rushed to their aid.

"The bishop of Bucharest and the Romanian government have asked me to open a house for children with AIDS. In a few days I shall go there with four Sisters and a doctor. I have already opened centers for the care of AIDS patients in New York, Washington, D.C., and San Francisco. This will be our first house of this type in Europe."

"It has been said that AIDS is a divine punishment for homosexuality and drug addiction. Do you think so, Mother Teresa?"

"No, it is not a divine punishment. Many people have contracted it without any fault of their own. There is a Sister who was infected as the result of a blood transfusion and she died little by little. We cannot judge; a simple injection or a contaminated syringe can transmit the disease. The greatest tragedy is that of the infants who contract AIDS from a father or mother.

"The children of lepers, on the contrary, are not born with leprosy. They are protected in the womb of the mother because the bacillus of leprosy cannot penetrate the placenta. But they can contract leprosy after birth through constant contact with the mother. Consequently, it is necessary to take them away from the mother immediately after birth, while they are still in good health, even before they can receive a kiss from their mother. We separate them from the family and keep them under constant medical surveillance in one of our centers. It is painful to have to do this, but it is necessary if we are to save them. The parents understand this and they make this sacrifice for the good of their children.

"But the AIDS virus can be transmitted even in the womb of the mother. Infants born with AIDS are destined not to survive. We care for them as best we can; we hold them in our arms and at least we baptize them before they die."

* * * * *

From Bucharest, Mother Teresa plans to go directly to Tirana, the capital of Albania. "I am Albanian by blood and by origin," she had said in the pithy autobiography she had given to the journalists in Oslo. She will be returning to her people and will again hear the language that she has almost forgotten under the layers of English, Hindu and Bengali. She will at last realize the dream of returning home, which is usually the dream of most emigrants, refugees and foreign missionaries. Mother Teresa had been away from her roots for more than 60 years, and yet she is the most famous Albanian in the whole world.

"Has it been your dream to return to Albania, Mother Teresa?"

She answers without any trace of sentimentality or nostalgia: "No, it has not been my dream. I don't have anybody down there. It is Albania that needs something, so I am not going there because it is my country, but in order to bring Christ there. Albania is by law an atheistic country. It is now the only country in the world that has written atheism into its Constitution. There are no churches, no mosques, no synagogues. The church buildings have been transformed into museums; the priests are imprisoned; nothing remains. My arrival will be the first step."

"How is that, Mother?"

"Because I never open a house unless it has a chapel. And in the chapel I place the crucifix. If they accept one of my houses, they also accept Christ, and in order to accept him, they have to change their laws. I have written to the President of Albania. He has not yet replied, but I know that he respects me."

"Do you always get what you want, Mother Teresa?"

"No, not always. The success of my work would not have been possible from a human point of view. As of now we are present in 90 countries and we have 420 houses. That's something great, isn't it? Especially for the younger generation it is a tremendous thing. The young are hungry for God. That is the grandeur of youth."

"What is your secret, Mother Teresa?"

"Prayer that leads to action. The fruit of prayer is faith. The fruit of faith is love. The fruit of love is service. See, it is all connected. What we do is the love of God in action."

"Mystical and practical; ascetical and administrative; Martha and Mary."

"We are contemplatives in action," she repeats. "I have said previously: when there is no longer any poor person, then we shall dedicate ourselves entirely to prayer. But I can hardly imagine that such a time will come. Jesus said: 'The poor you have always with you'."

In addition to her innate ability to state things succinctly and in their essence, Mother Teresa has a gift for using the appropriate gesture. Now she takes one of my hands and touches every finger as she repeats these five words: *You did it to me*.

Touching my little finger, she says: *You*; then the ring finger, *did*; then the middle finger, *it*; then the index finger, *to*; and finally the thumb, *me*. She repeats it with the patience of a mother teaching her child. "You did it to me. Did you save the life of an infant? You did it to me. Did you feed a hungry person? You did it to me." Mother laughs reassuringly: "It's all very simple, and yet it is often forgotten."

"Is it truly so simple to become a saint?"

"Yes, it is simple. Your vocation is to write, isn't it? Well, if you don't write lies, if you don't write things that debase people, you can become a very holy person. What you write can be transformed into prayer."

"People say that you are the only living saint, Mother Teresa."

"Oh no; every person was created to become a saint. We were all created for the same purpose: to love and to be loved. We were created for great things. God manifests his greatness by using our nothingness. That is very evident. I am happy that you see Jesus in me, because I see him in you."

Through the window under the trellis that covers the corridor come the sounds of a bell and the footsteps of the Sisters. The hour of evening adoration is about to begin and the Sisters are hastening to the chapel. Mother looks at me in silence and delicately lets me know that it is time for me to depart. But there is still something that has weighed on my mind since I arrived. I must tell Mother Teresa that misfortune has fallen upon my home and that I am so bowed down with suffering that

I find it very difficult to lift my head and look to the future. Mother Teresa listens to me in silence. She tells me to discuss the matter calmly, since she still has time to listen to me. Then she tells me what I needed to hear: "Suffering is a gift from God for you. Suffering is a marvelous gift. I pray that you will not frustrate the work of the Lord, that you will not spoil what is the Lord's work and not ours."

HOME AT LAST

There are no religious symbols in the cemetery at Tirana, the capital of Albania. Muslims, Christians, Jews and agnostics are all equal, even in death, because according to Article 37 of the Albanian Constitution, the country is officially atheistic. Only on two gravestones, somewhat distant from one another, are there bronze crosses, and they are very new. It is evident that they have been there only a short time. Mother Teresa had them placed over the graves of her mother and her sister.

The cemetery is in Kombinat, a suburb of Tirana. In the surrounding hills there are concrete bunkers, constructed by the dictator Enver Hoxha, who was obsessed with the fear of encirclement or foreign invasion. With rhetorical flair he called them "the immobile armed tanks of the people, which never attack and never retreat." There are 800,000 such bunkers throughout Albania and they are connected with an intricate system of subterraneous passages. They cost a dizzying amount, paid for by the treasury of a country that has three million poor people.

There is no photo on the gravestone of her mother Drane, but only the dates of her birth and death, 1889-1972. There is also a simple inscription: "*Ne Shenj Kujtimi* (A sign of remembrance), with the signature: Lazri and Gonxha. Lazri is Albanian for Lazar, the brother of Mother Teresa, and Gonxha is Mother

Teresa's childhood pet name. The same writing is found on the tombstone of Age, Mother Teresa's sister, with the dates, 1913-1973. There is also a photo of a beautiful face with a proud and direct look. Near the grave there is a sweet-briar bush.

Mother Teresa is carrying two bouquets of yellow flowers and some branches of laurel. She wears a blue sweater draped over her shoulders because the 1991 springtime is unseasonably chilly. She places the flowers on the graves, lightly caresses the tombstones, and then remains a long time in prayer with her forehead resting on her joined hands.

* * * * *

Mother Teresa suffered the pain of never again seeing her mother and sister since she left home to enter the convent in Ireland at the age of 18. In the years before World War II there was no opportunity to leave India. After the war the Albanian government, which was first Stalinist, then Maoist, and finally a strong bulwark of the strictest and purest Marxism, would not permit Mother Teresa to enter Albania or her mother and sister to leave.

"I want to see you before I die," her mother had said in a letter. "This is the only grace I ask of God." In Italy Mother Teresa's brother Lazar had tried every possible diplomatic channel to obtain visas for his mother and sister. The only reply he ever received was: "Drane and Age Bojaxhiu are not in sufficiently good physical condition to make a journey to a foreign country." Lazar had commented: "It's a shame. The only sickness of my mother and Age is called loneliness and despair. They are being buried alive."

In her book, *Such a Vision of the Street*, Eileen Egan describes one of the many unsuccessful efforts of Mother Teresa to get her mother and sister out of Albania:

> Mother Teresa made a desperate attempt to have
> Drane and Age come to Italy by going in person to see

the Albanians. We made our way to the Albanian Embassy and found it a building shuttered and silent as a tomb. There was no sign of life even after we had rung a loud bell three times. At last a man with a broad face and surprised blue eyes opened the door. He was evidently not accustomed to visitors... Mother Teresa fastened her tawny eyes on him and said simply in her native tongue: "*Sou de Schipteru*" (I am from Albania). This was literally correct, since she could no longer say she was Albanian, having acquired Indian citizenship.

The Embassy employee looked from Mother Teresa to me as though unable to credit his senses and then said a few brusque words which we took to be an invitation to enter the building. He preceded us into a dark, shuttered parlor.

The three of us settled into the large dark chairs around a low coffee table and Mother Teresa said once more: "*Sou de Schipteru*."

The man replied with a burst of speech while Mother Teresa struggled to form a few words. A blush rose covered her face; she turned to me, smiling ruefully. "I can't find the words in my mother tongue. It's too far back."

At that point I thought I had better explain our presence, since the Albanian was looking uneasy..., I explained that the woman who had come to see him was from an Albanian family.... I pointed out that although she had become an Indian citizen, her origin was known and she had brought great honor to Albania.

The Albanian's face lit up at my rather shameless appeal to nationalism. Mother Teresa asked him if he spoke Serbo-Croatian. He did, and from then on Mother Teresa told her own tale. The man listened eagerly and, at one point, raised his large hand to his face and wiped away tears that streamed from his eyes....

He asked for more details of the work in Calcutta.... "I will do my best for her. I will explain to the attaché, and you must come back tomorrow at the same hour." He talked to Mother Teresa in Serbo-Croatian as he walked us to the door.

The following day the attaché was waiting for us.... He promised to get in touch with the government in Tirana.

On Friday morning we went again to the Albanian Embassy and this time were met by another staff member. The attaché, he explained, was *"fuori Roma"* (away from Rome). He told Mother Teresa that he had no news for her about the exit visa.... Though there were more calls to the Albanian Embassy, no exit visas were ever issued. In two years Drane Bojaxhiu was dead. A few years later, Age followed her in death.

* * * * *

In the kitchen of a tiny apartment in Tirana, Glystina and Tolo Zhupa offer me a cup of strong Turkish coffee and a small glass of Scanderbeg, a sweet wine flavored with cloves, as they talk to me about Drane and Age Bojaxhiu. They had known them well because they had been neighbors in a new section of Tirana called "Friendship Block" during the time that Albania was on friendly terms with the Soviet Union. Drane and Age lived alone in poverty. They always had flowers on their balcony. Drane still kept a trunk filled with things that belonged to Lazar, who was living in Italy. It contained clothing, personal effects and even a small rug. When they asked Drane: "Why don't you use them?" she replied somewhat gruffly: "No, they will be useful to Lazar when he returns."

Age worked as an announcer for Radio Tirana in the section for the Serbo-Croatian language. But when the government enforced one of its recurring restrictions against "the enemies of the Socialist State," Age was dismissed. She was guilty of being the sister of Lazar Bojaxhiu, who was on the black list of Albanians who had taken refuge in Italy, and of Agnes Bojaxhiu, a Catholic nun known as Mother Teresa of Calcutta.

Age then began working as a seamstress in her own home, but she had to do it secretly because all private business was forbidden by the government. Whenever a letter arrived from India, usually taking months to do so, Drane would run to read it to her neighbors, Glystina and Tolo. "I cannot do anything else for you but pray," wrote Mother Teresa; and to her sister she wrote: "Age, you are our Mama's guardian angel."

At Easter and at Christmas Drane and Age would prepare the traditional food of Albanian Christians and then invite Glystina, who was Catholic, and Tolo, who was Orthodox. At Christmas they had *sarma*, cabbage leaves stuffed with rice. At Easter they prepared *buke e Pashkeve*, the Easter bread made with flour and milk but without sugar, and garnished with the long green onions of springtime and hard-boiled eggs dyed red. There was one colored egg for each person, plus an extra egg for the unexpected guest, according to Albanian custom. The bread was prepared on Holy Saturday and then taken to the church to be blessed by the priest at the Easter Vigil.

In 1967 the government enforced severe laws against religion. All the churches were closed, priests were expelled or imprisoned, and even the colored Easter eggs were forbidden. Anyone who dared to carry on the Easter tradition had to do so secretly, like Christians in the days of the catacombs. It even had to be kept secret from the children in the family, lest they talk about it outside the home. And the red shells of the Easter eggs that were eaten secretly could not be thrown into the garbage;

they had to be burned. A piece of the shell found by a neighbor who is an informant could result in being accused of "anti-Socialist activity and propaganda," for which the punishment could be six years in prison.

"You are the first person to whom we have told these things," said Glystina and Tolo. He, a pensioned bank clerk, and she, a bookkeeper for a construction firm, live comfortably in a nice apartment. Their two children are now settled with their own families. When they were little, the children were very lively and sometimes Drane would become a bit irritated when, from her balcony she saw them fighting with other children on the street. She would knock on the wall between the two apartments and call to Glystina: "Hurry, before the other children hurt them."

* * * * *

After the long winter of dictatorship, springtime came to Tirana. The students knocked down the huge statue of Enver Hoxha that dominated the Scanderbeg Plaza, clothed in a bronze cape, his glance facing eastward toward the rising sun. The museum containing an exhibition of the works of his regime is closed "for repairs," and there is a move to turn it into a discotheque. The campus of the university has been re-baptized Democracy Plaza and the Democratic Party has its meetings there. This party came into being, together with five other political parties, when President Ramiz Alia introduced the multi-party system. People then voted in the first free election in the history of Albania.

In Calcutta, Mother Teresa learned that Albania was finally free. She then opened churches and established two houses of the Missionaries of Charity, one at Tirana and another at Scutari. During the Mass she prayed in the midst of a huge crowd and the people rushed forward to touch her. On March 19, the feast of St. Joseph, she baptized many infants, and among them, Glystina's niece Viola, the daughter of her brother Edward Joni. However, on that joyful day Glystina experienced a slight disappointment.

"St. Anthony's Church was crowded and I couldn't get close to Mother Teresa. She had poured the water over the heads of the infants and had recited the formula of baptism; then she was surrounded by the crowd. I was so overcome that I didn't have the strength to make my way to her and tell her that I was a friend of her mother and sister."

The Franciscan Fathers were in charge of St. Anthony's Parish. When it was closed in 1967, as were all the churches and mosques in Albania, it was transformed into the center for the Pioneers, the Communist youth organization. Mother Teresa succeeded in having the church reopened and the former pastor, Father Zef Plumi, reinstated. He was a man in his seventies, bent over and drained of strength after 23 years of imprisonment and forced labor. "But now those times have passed and God has once again turned his eyes toward us."

This is the account given by Father Zef: "Four pastors in Tirana were arrested in 1967, and I was one of them. They accused us of high treason, spies for the Italian Embassy. A few months later, two of them were shot, Father Zef Bici and Father Mark Dushi. Father Mark and I had been sentenced to 28 years in prison, and in the first years I was punished with forced labor in the chromium mines at Spac. That is where they sent the stubborn prisoners who would not confess to anything.

"Then I was sent to work at draining the swamp at Narta, near Valona in the south. It was a very unhealthy place infested with mosquitoes. During the day we carried earth to the swamp, but during the night it was again covered with water, so we had to start all over again the next day. It was a labor of Sisyphus. With our own hands we constructed a dam seven kilometers long and six meters wide. Our daily rations were supposed to consist of 7 grams of olive oil, 60 grams of macaroni, 170 grams of vegetables, 15 grams of sugar, 800 grams of bread and 40 grams of meat. The meat was held back, however, because I never saw any of it. If anyone protested, there was a prison within the prison, an infernal place of solitary confinement. Sometimes I was tempted to doubt my faith, but I consoled myself by thinking that in the Garden of Gethsemane Jesus was also tempted, so I managed to struggle through.

In prison I met the most honorable men in Albania and also the most dishonorable. The most honorable were the innocent ones who bore their unjust condemnation with dignity and courage; the most dishonorable were the spies who were placed among us as cell-mates so that they could win our trust and our confidence. We got into the habit of never speaking to anybody."

The first thing that Father Zef did when Mother Teresa told him to take back possession of his church was to recover the church bell and attach it to an acacia tree in the courtyard. He planned eventually to restore it to the church tower, which at the time was partially collapsed.

The church bell had also been accustomed to keep silence during those difficult years. To prevent it from being seized by the government and melted down, it had been removed at night and hidden by a Muslim house-painter, Fiqri Muho, a friend of Father Zef. Fiqri had kept it buried in his cellar for 12 years, but when he had to move to another house, he entrusted it to Gjergii Komino, an Orthodox Christian who was a professor of ethnology. The professor ended up in prison because he had written a "revolutionary" tract. Eventually Fiqri Muho was also imprisoned because he had publicly complained about the scarcity of potatoes.

Thus, all three ended up in prison — the Franciscan friar, the Muslim house-painter, and the Orthodox Christian professor. Fortunately, they were all sent to the same prison. They knew each other well and they trusted each other. Perhaps they spoke about the church bell because that hidden bell became a symbol of freedom, of life outside the prison, of a time when they would once again live like free men, without oppression and fear.

* * * * *

It is Easter, 1991, the first Easter in a free Albania in 45 years. Mother Teresa is travelling around the country as free as a bird. She opens a house in Tirana at Number 35 Ali Pasha, which was formerly the home of the mayor, and another house at Number 27 Ali Gusija, next to St. Anthony's Church, which had been used as the center for Communist youth. She also re-opens the Cathedral of the Sacred Heart, which had been turned into a movie theater named *Kinarinia,*

At midnight on Holy Saturday, 1991, I follow Mother Teresa into the cathedral for the liturgy of the Easter Vigil. The celebrant is Father George Gjergji, who had formerly been pastor at Pec in Kosovo and had taken refuge in Italy to escape from the Communist regime. Mother Teresa found him at St. Joseph's Parish in Grottaferrata, outside of Rome. In a few days she arranged for him to receive a passport, a visa and a plane ticket from Rome to Tirana.

In the cathedral people are jostling with one another to get close to Mother Teresa. The walls smell of fresh paint but the floor still bears the scuff marks of shoes because there had not been time to clean it. The flame from the Paschal candle is reflected in the gold of the chalice and paten, gifts to Mother Teresa from Pope John Paul II.

Mother Teresa is up close to the altar with ten of her Missionaries of Charity, all of whom are foreigners except Sister Ancilla, who is Albanian. The Mass is being celebrated in Albanian, and Father George asks the people to respond. The only ones who do so are Mother Teresa and Sister Ancilla. The rest of the Sisters know the responses, but they cannot speak Albanian; the people know Albanian, but they do not know the responses. There are no pews, so the people remain standing, moving slightly with their collective breathing. They have placed near the altar their *buke e Pashkeve*, the Easter bread, the boiled eggs dyed red and some green onions. There are also some packets containing a piece of white cheese. Father George blesses all the food and then the women come forward to reclaim their items.

* * * * *

Before leaving Tirana I went to say good-bye to Mother Teresa at Number 35 Ali Pasha, the former home of the mayor. The house was built in 1939, when the Italians occupied Albania and there was much traffic between Tirana and Rome. One of the Sisters asked me to wait in the garden because at the moment Mother Teresa was speaking with the Minister of Health. From my seat under the vine-covered trellis, now bare, I can see white-haired people looking out the windows on the second floor. Some twenty elderly women are cared for in this house.

Finally Mother Teresa comes out, but she gives me a signal to wait a moment. Then she goes to the garden gate, where a small group of people is waiting. She distributes some religious medals to them and then comes toward me with a polite smile. I interpret the smile as a reminder to me of the number of times I have interrupted her in her work. Her first words are an affectionate complaint: "You are always writing." Then she resigns herself to answering my questions.

"Are you happy to be home, Mother Teresa?"

"Yes, I am happy. But the poor are everywhere — Tirana, New York, Rome."

"Have you received support here in Albania?"

"Everybody helps me, and especially the authorities. But I am not the one who prompts people's help; it is the poor. The poor are the magnet. The poor are the connection between us and God. I am only the pencil with which God writes what he wants."

"What do you think of the first free election?"

"You know that I do not talk politics."

"But will Albania change?"

"It will change, with your help and mine. Yes, your help is also important, if you begin to pray in your family."

"What will you do now, Mother Teresa?"

"I shall remain in Albania for a few more days. I am going to open a house for infants in Scutari."

Mother Teresa takes a medal from her shopping bag and kisses it before giving it to me. She takes my hands in her warm and gnarled hands and brings me up to date on her progress, as I have heard her do so many times before.

"With the two houses in Tirana and the one in Scutari, I shall have 443 houses in 95 countries."

I know that the numbers will have increased by the time of our next interview, and she will tell me about it as she always does. There will be another house in another country. It will be necessary to write new names and new places in the atlas of charity.

AFTER MOTHER TERESA?

What will happen to the Missionaries of Charity after Mother Teresa? Who will take her place at the head of the Congregation?

In answering these questions, Mother Teresa sometimes responds in a manner that is somewhat fatalistic: "If my work is of God, he will take care of it. Otherwise, it will be well for it to disappear." But more often she will say: "There will be no problem. God will know how to find a person more humble, more obedient, more faithful, more little, with a more profound faith, and through that person he will do greater works." It is useless to ask her who this person is who has so much "more." And within the Congregation it is almost a kind of blasphemy to mention "after Mother Teresa." She is the foundress; she is the one who has personified the philosophy and charism of the Missionaries of Charity; she is the one who has personally selected each one of her thousands of Sisters; she is the one who has animated the entire Congregation with her unifying and inimitable spirit.

Mother Teresa does not govern the Congregation alone; there is a General Council composed of six Sisters who assist her in the various aspects of administration: the foundation of new houses, the appointment of superiors, keeping financial accounts, maintaining contact with benefactors, the formation of novices and Sisters in temporary vows. It is possible that the new superior general will be chosen from these six Sisters who work in very close contact with Mother Teresa.

The most "papabile" seems to be Sister Agnes Das, the first follower of Mother Teresa. She is a short, taciturn Bengali, a former student of Mother Teresa at the school conducted by the Sisters of Loreto at Entally. She joined Mother Teresa in 1949 and at present she holds the office of Assistant General.

Sister Priscilla Lewis, an Anglo-Indian from Shillong in northeast India, is the Secretary General and has charge of public relations for the Congregation. She was formerly a teacher and she joined the Missionaries of Charity in 1957.

Sister Shanti D'Souza is a native of Goa. She has a degree in science and formerly worked for the multinational corporation Glaxo of Bombay. She entered the Congregation in 1956 and Mother Teresa sent her to study medicine at Calcutta Medical College. She works as a medical doctor and also has charge of the formation of the Sisters who are in the last year before final religious profession.

Sister Camillus Pereira comes from Bangalore. She entered the Congregation in 1960 and is the youngest member of the General Council. She is an economist and was formerly employed by a company in Bombay. For 23 years she has been in charge of the finances of the Congregation as well as relations with organizations in foreign countries and benefactors in general. At present she is the superior of all the houses in Calcutta.

Sister Dorothy Francis, from Bengal, was the fourth person to join the Missionaries of Charity. She is also a former student of Mother Teresa at Entally and she entered the Congregation in 1950. For many years she worked in Australia and in Latin America. Now she assists in the formation of the Sisters in the year prior to their final religious profession.

Sister Andrea Bonk is the only Westerner on the General Council. She is from Germany and she joined the Missionaries of Charity in 1959. She also studied medicine at the Calcutta

Medical College and has worked as a doctor in the United States and in the Philippines. She is highly regarded for her administrative ability.

The decision as to who will succeed Mother Teresa as Superior General is reached by the entire Congregation by free and secret vote. According to the Constitutions of the Missionaries of Charity, the Superior General must be at least 40 years of age and at least 10 years in final religious profession. The term of office is six years, and she can be re-elected only once. When Mother Teresa was re-elected in 1960, it was necessary to obtain the approval of the Holy See for a dispensation from the Constitutions of the Congregation. [*Translator's note*: When there is a limit to successive terms of office, as in the Constitutions of the Missionaries of Charity, the general law of the Church allows the process called "postulation." At least two-thirds of the membership must vote for the individual and the postulation must then be approved by the proper ecclesiastical authority. Cf. *The Code of Canon Law*, canons 180-183.]

The Indian journalist, Payal Singh, published an article in the Italian magazine, *Mondo e Missione* in the June-July issue of 1990. He points out what he considers a special difficulty in finding suitable superiors in the Missionaries of Charity:

> Mother Teresa has problems in finding superiors in her order. Unlike most other religious congregations, which are involved in teaching, the Missionaries of Charity do not stress education and formation in the selection of candidates. What they require is a smiling face and cheerful availability. The majority of the novices have not even completed high school. Their greatest asset is that they are willing to live a life of great sacrifice with joy.
>
> Mother Teresa is truly the epicenter of the Congregation. For that reason it will not be easy to hold

the young Sisters together after she retires. The new Superior General will have to measure up, not to a person, but to an ideal.

The "after Mother Teresa" is once again in the hands of God. Article 22 of the Constitutions states: "We should leave to almighty God every future project. Yesterday is gone, tomorrow has not yet come, and we have only today to know, love and serve Jesus."

Mother Teresa always repeats this, word for word, whenever anyone asks her about her projects for the future. She always says: "I live day by day. Yesterday is past. Tomorrow has not yet come. I have only today to love Jesus."

BIBLIOGRAPHY

Hundreds of books have been written about Mother Teresa and her work. The following are the best known and the most useful for American readers:

MALCOM MUGGERIDGE, *Something Beautiful for God*, Harper & Row, New York, 1971. The author was a well-known journalist and is the first Westerner to make Mother Teresa known outside of India.

DESMOND DOIG, *Mother Teresa: Her People and her Work*, Harper & Row, New York, 1976. A journalist for *The Calcutta Statesman*, Desmond Doig wrote the first articles about Mother Teresa in India. This book is beautifully illustrated.

EILEEN EGAN, *Such a Vision of the Street: Mother Teresa — The Spirit and the Work*, Doubleday & Company, Garden City, N.Y., 1985. A great friend and collaborator of Mother Teresa, Eileen Egan worked for the Catholic Relief Services. Her book is a treasury of first-hand information.

OMER TANGHE, *For the Least of My Brothers: The Spirituality of Mother Teresa and Catherine Doherty*, Alba House, New York, 1989. Insights into the spirituality of Mother Teresa by a priest who knew her well and was often invited to give conferences to her Sisters in Calcutta.